Romans

Romans

Good News
that Changes
Everything

A Bible Study by

MELISSA SPOELSTRA

Abingdon Women

Nashville

Romans
Good News that Changes Everything

Copyright © 2019 Abingdon Press
All rights reserved.

ISBN 978-1-5018-3897-2

19 20 21 22 23 24 25 26 27 28 — 10 9 8 7 6 5 4 3 2 1
MANUFACTURED IN THE UNITED STATES OF AMERICA

Special thanks to the gals who piloted this study with me. They received very rough chapters and gave critical feedback to sharpen the content. I appreciate the way they engaged their minds and hearts in studying Romans with discernment and shared their ideas within the group. Thank you so much, Becky Bess, Chrissy, Deb, Denise, Jean, Marybeth, Melissa, Nori, Rindy, and Tanya.

I'm grateful for each one of you and treasure you as my sharpening "irons." Many will benefit from your insights, corrections, and creativity.

Contents

About the Author

Melissa Spoelstra is a popular women's conference speaker (including the Aspire Women's Events), Bible teacher, and author who is madly in love with Jesus and passionate about studying God's Word and helping women of all ages seek Christ and know Him more intimately through serious Bible study. Having a degree in Bible theology, she enjoys teaching God's Word to the body of Christ, traveling to diverse groups and churches across the United States and also to Nairobi, Kenya, for a women's prayer conference. Melissa is the author of the Bible studies *Elijah: Spiritual Stamina in Every Season, Numbers: Learning Contentment in a Culture of More, First Corinthians: Living Love When We Disagree, Joseph: The Journey to Forgiveness,* and *Jeremiah: Daring to Hope in an Unstable World* and the books *Dare to Hope: Living Intentionally in an Unstable World, Total Family Makeover: 8 Practical Steps to Making Disciples at Home,* and *Total Christmas Makeover: 31 Devotions to Celebrate with Purpose.* She is a regular contributor to the Proverbs 31 First Five App and the Girlfriends in God online daily devotional. She has published articles in *ParentLife, Women's Spectrum,* and *Just Between Us* and writes her own regular blog in which she shares her musings about what God is teaching her on any given day. Melissa lives in Pickerington, Ohio, with her pastor husband, Sean, and their four kids: Zach, Abby, Sara, and Rachel.

Follow Melissa:

@MelSpoelstra

@Daring2Hope

@Author MelissaSpoelstra

Her blog   MelissaSpoelstra.com

(check here also for event dates and booking information)

Introduction to This Study

Bad news surrounds us. It comes through our computer and television screens with reports of natural disasters, violence, and tragedy. We encounter it in doctors' offices, strained relationships, and home or car repairs. And when those we love receive bad news, it compounds our personal pile of woes.

All of this bad news can overwhelm us and cause us to plead with Jesus to return . . . like today! In the midst of our complicated lives, we can drift toward cynicism, fear, or despair. As followers of Jesus, we need constant reminders that through all of our trials, we carry treasured good news for a broken planet.

Sin separates us from God, but Jesus came and laid down His life to reconcile us with God (2 Corinthians 5:18). Through Him we can have a relationship with the Creator of the universe. This is the gospel, which literally means "good news." As we study Romans over the next six weeks, we will mine the richness of this good news. The truths we will explore won't necessarily provide a quick fix for all the bad news in our lives, but they will give us perspective to reframe the bad news and remind us of our hope for the future.

This letter that the apostle Paul wrote to the church at Rome has been a source of spiritual transformation and renewal throughout church history, impacting the lives of important leaders such as Saint Augustine, John Chrysostom, Martin Luther, John Calvin, John Wesley, Jonathan Edwards, Karl Barth, and many others. In fact, Luther acknowledged its power for all of us when he said, "We can never read it or ponder over it too much, for the more we deal with it, the more precious it becomes and the better it tastes."[1] When we read and study this timeless letter, we cannot help being affected personally.

So, I invite you to join me in rediscovering the good news in your life through Paul's Letter to the Romans. Whether this is your first time through its pages or you've been a student of its truths for decades, get ready for transformation in your thinking, attitudes, and actions. Warren Wiersbe has said, "If you are tired of all the wrong things in your life, in the lives of others, and in this world, then Paul's epistle to the Romans is the book for you."[2]

Digging into Romans will require more than a cursory skimming. We cannot swallow the information whole or choke it down. We will want to chew on it. This will mean thinking and meditating on it, questioning it, discussing it alongside other believers, and

even memorizing some of it. Only then will we be able to properly digest its contents and perhaps encounter the spiritual renewal that so many before us have detailed in their studies of Romans.

So much has been written about Romans that I wondered whether more needed to be said. As I wrestled through this question, I resonated with one commentator who writes, "Each new generation deserves a fresh hearing of this ancient masterpiece."[3] As we read the Bible today, we ask different questions from different angles; so we need to continually revisit the truths found in Paul's longest letter. My prayer is that this study will help you do just that, bringing great hope and spiritual renewal into the practical realities of your own life.

Each week in our study we will cover two to three chapters of Romans. We will be highlighting significant concepts regarding the good news about six topics: faith, hope, daily life, God's plan, relationships, and eternity. I don't know what bad news you have received this week, but I do know that as we make this journey together, we will continually find good news to encourage and transform us.

Options for Study

Before beginning the study, I invite you to consider the level of commitment your time and life circumstances will allow. I have found that what I put into a Bible study directly correlates to what I get out of it. When I commit to do the homework daily, God's truths sink deeper as I take time to reflect and meditate on what God is teaching me. When I am intentional about gathering with other women to watch videos and have discussion, I find that this helps keep me from falling off the Bible study wagon midway. Also, making a point to memorize verses and dig deeper by looking at additional materials greatly benefits my soul.

At other times, however, I have bitten off more than I can chew. When our faith is new, our children are small, or there are great demands on our time because of difficult circumstances or challenges, we need to be realistic about what we will be able to finish. So this study is designed with options that enable you to tailor it for your particular circumstances and needs.

1. **Basic Study.** The basic study includes five daily readings or lessons. Each lesson combines study of Scripture with personal reflection and application (boldface type indicates write-in-the-book questions and activities), ending with a suggestion for talking with God about what you've learned and a "Big Idea" or takeaway from the lesson. On average you will need about twenty to thirty minutes to complete each lesson.

At the end of each week, you will find a Weekly Wrap Up to guide you in a quick review of what you've learned. You don't want to skip this part, which you'll find to be one of the most practical tools of the study. This brief exercise will help your take-aways from the lessons "stick," making a real and practical difference in your daily life.

When you gather with your group to review each week's material, you will watch a video, discuss what you are learning, and pray together. I encourage you to discuss the insights you are gaining and how God is working in your own life.

2. Deeper Study. If you want an even deeper study, there is a memory verses for each week (you'll find a memorization exercise at the end of each lesson) plus optional "Digging Deeper" articles available at abingdonwomen.com/Romans. These articles are second level, more academic looks at some of the themes we didn't have the space to tackle in the regular flow of the study (for example, circumcision, baptism, essentials and nonessentials, and so on).

3. Lighter Commitment. If you are in a season of life in which you need a lighter commitment, I encourage you to give yourself permission to do what you can. God will bless your efforts and speak to you through this study at every level of participation.

Take time now to pray and decide which study option is right for you, and check it below.

___ 1. Basic Study
___ 2. Deeper Study
___ 3. Lighter Commitment: I will_____.

Be sure to let someone in your group know which option you have chosen to do so that you have some accountability and encouragement.

A Final Word

Will you join me in taking a posture of listening and learning as we approach this powerful book packed with good news? Let's ask God to do a mighty work in and through us as we study so that we might be inspired with a spiritual renewal that spreads to those around us!

Melissa

Introductory Background

Authorship and Date

The apostle Paul's authorship of the book is largely undisputed (Romans 1:1). He likely wrote this letter to the Romans while visiting the church at Corinth.[1] Most scholars agree that Paul wrote the letter somewhere between AD 55 and 58, on his third missionary trip.[2]

Paul's scribe who wrote down the actual words of the letter was named Tertius (Romans 16:22).

Purpose

Paul stated in his letter that he was planning to bring a financial gift to the church in Jerusalem before visiting the church in Rome, with later plans to bring the gospel to Spain.

Opinions differ on the exact purpose of the letter. While we will not go into detail about the many theories, here are a few representative views of various Bible commentators:

- Paul's letter explains justification by faith for the purpose of encouraging unity between the Gentiles (non-Jews) and Jewish believers.[3]
- The theme is salvation by faith, which brings life.[4]
- Romans is about the righteousness of God.[5]
- The letter is Paul's "official doctrinal statement" intended to introduce him to the church in Rome and win their support for evangelism to the nations.[6]

It seems that Paul did not have one overriding motive in writing his letter but several, as we see throughout the sixteen chapters. We cannot discuss Paul's motive or purpose without mentioning the debate among scholars regarding the individual versus corporate nature of this letter to the church at Rome. Many have highlighted the concept of a personal relationship with God found within its chapters. Luther's question, for example, was, "How can a sinner get right with a wrathful God?" Critics of this focus on the individual emphasize the corporate mindset of society during biblical times. I appreciate one commentator's view that both individual and corporate themes are interwoven in the letter, highlighting how the gospel or good news impacts people personally and in group contexts.[7]

Key Verse

For I am not ashamed of this Good News about Christ. It is the power of God at work, saving everyone who believes—the Jew first and also the Gentile. This Good News tells us how God makes us right in his sight. This is accomplished from start to finish by faith. As the Scriptures say, "It is through faith that a righteous person has life."

(Romans 1:16-17)

Audience

Paul wrote this letter to the Roman church, which probably met in as many as five house or tenement churches (Romans 16:5, 10-11, 14-15). One commentator suggests that the total attendance would perhaps have been a few hundred since a large house church could accommodate fifty people for worship.[8]

Relevance

Romans is dripping with references to the Hebrew Scriptures, which comprise a large part of our Old Testament—fifty-seven times Paul quotes from them. This shows us continuity between the Old and New Testaments and highlights Christ's fulfillment of both the law and prophecies. We glimpse Christ as the Jewish Messiah who offers His grace to all—including Gentiles.

The theological and practical importance of the book for every Christian is captured in some of the descriptors it has been given. Contemporary commentators refer to Romans as:

- The Christian Magna Carta[9]
- The first systematic theology of the Christian faith[10]
- The chief part of the New Testament[11]
- Paul's magnum opus[12]
- Paul's spiritual trumpet[13]
- The Constitution of Universal Christianity[14]
- The most important of Paul's writings[15]

Wow! I hope these references of significance don't cause you to think that Romans is too lofty to be accessible. Throughout our study I believe you will resonate with the truths we'll discover about God and people. My prayer is that you will personally encounter the good news that changes everything in your life!

Week 1

Good News About Faith

Romans 1–3

Memory Verse

¹⁶For I am not ashamed of this Good News about Christ. It is the power of God at work, saving everyone who believes—the Jew first and also the Gentile. ¹⁷This Good News tells us how God makes us right in his sight. This is accomplished from start to finish by faith. As the Scriptures say, "It is through faith that a righteous person has life."

(Romans 1:16-17)

DAY 1: THE POWER

As we begin our study through the letter to the Romans, I wonder what images today's title conjures up in your mind. Perhaps you are feeling powerful. I feel this way when I exercise self-control with chocolate, check things off my to-do list, or finish an extended time of prayer. Others of you might read the word *power* and question why a sense of powerlessness seems to pervade your life.

I can think of times when I've felt powerless. When my daughter cried herself to sleep because her hair was falling out in seventh grade due to the autoimmune disorder alopecia, I wished there was something I could do to make it better. When a friendship remained fractured after many repair attempts, I wanted a formula to fix it. Other times my inability to stick with a healthy eating plan, budget, or spiritual discipline reveals my struggle with self-control. Anyone else with me on this?

As we crack open the letter to the Romans, we will find reminders that we serve a powerful God who has good news for the people He created. This good news truly has the power to change everything in our lives. It may not erase all of the bad news or the powerlessness we feel in response to it, but God's good news can help us embrace H*is* power and reframe our difficulties in light of that.

Before we dig into the text, take a moment to consider your spiritual posture right now.

Are you resigned, indifferent, curious, expectant, or something else? Ask God to prepare you for our study and to show you His heart through His words in the Letter to the Romans. Pray silently or out loud, or write your prayer below:

Paul's Epistle to the Romans is the longest and most theological of his letters. Many of his other letters were written from prison or during times of personal duress, but Paul penned his letter to the church at Rome during a season of relative calm in his life while in Corinth during his third missionary journey (sometime between AD 55 and 58).[3] At this point in Paul's ministry he had been preaching about Christ for almost twenty-five years. He had a wealth of experience in church planting and had had to apply his theology in practical ministry. He wrote Romans at a time when he could reflect on his beliefs and share with the Roman Christians the important truths that would prove

Scripture Focus

Romans 1:1-17

Digging Deeper

What exactly did Paul mean when he called the believers in Rome "saints"? How does this word apply to believers today? Check out the Digging Deeper article for Week 1, "The Saints," to find out (see AbingdonWomen.com/Romans).

Extra Insight

Paul's letters are often referred to as epistles. An epistle is a letter, especially a formal one.[1] Traditionally thirteen letters are ascribed to Paul, though only seven of the thirteen are undisputed in authorship.[2]

Extra Insight

The word *gospel* is the Greek noun *euangelion* and means good news.[4]

foundational for church life. Knowing where Paul was in his life and ministry will aid us as we seek to interpret a letter that was intended for a specific audience during a particular time in history.

In order to cover the entire book in six sessions, we will not be able to study every verse in depth. Instead we will look for key ideas and themes that best help us understand and embrace the good news that changes everything.

In the very first section of Romans, we will find a greeting that was typical of ancient letters including a sender, recipient, and personal welcome.[5]

Read Romans 1:1-7 and identify each of these elements:

Sender (1:1)	
Recipients (1:7a)	
Summary of Greeting (1:7b)	

Fast Facts about Paul and the Roman Church

- Paul wrote more in his introduction to the church in Rome than in any other letter's opening words, likely because he didn't plant the Roman church and needed to spend more time developing an acquaintance.

- Paul had never visited the church at Rome at the time that he wrote this letter.

- We don't know for certain how the Roman church began, but some commentators suggest Roman Jews present at Pentecost (Acts 2:10) could have returned home to Rome and started the church.[6] Others mention that it may have been started by the partners in ministry that Paul met in other regions, who later traveled to Rome.[7]

- Paul eventually did make it to Rome, but he came in chains when he appealed to Caesar after his arrest in Jerusalem (Acts 28:11-17). He lived under house arrest with a guard but was able to interact with believers in his home in Rome.

This is Paul's longest introduction of any letter perhaps because he felt he needed a greater introduction since he wasn't readily known to the congregation. Paul didn't plant the church at Rome and had never been able to visit it. We don't really know how the Roman church began.

How did Paul describe himself in verse 1?

By calling himself a servant or slave (*doulos*) of Christ, Paul emphasizes his humility in belonging to Christ; but he tempers that with authority when he says he has been chosen by God to be an apostle. Right off the bat, he mentions the good news promised by the prophets. In this way, Paul establishes that God's new plan isn't so new. In fact, it is a fulfillment of the original plan to save us.

Skim back through verses 1-7 and look for the word *power*. According to verse 4, whose power is it, and how was it used?

Now read Romans 8:11 in the margin, and describe how this power relates to a believer in Christ:

The Spirit of God, who raised Jesus from the dead, lives in you. And just as God raised Christ Jesus from the dead, he will give life to your mortal bodies by this same Spirit living within you.
(Romans 8:11)

If you are a follower of Christ, the Holy Spirit resides within you, giving you the same power that raised Jesus from the grave. When I think about all the difficulties in life, that truth encourages the socks off me. People I love get diseases, conflicts in relationships are inevitable, and events beyond my control abound. However, I am not a victim of my circumstances. I have the power of God living inside me to help me through all the brokenness in this world.

I hope the reality of the Holy Spirit's power in your life sinks deep into your soul today as you consider any area of your life where you have been feeling powerless. You have resurrection power living inside you. Now that is some good news for this day!

Write a brief sentence of thanks to God for this power:

Read Romans 1:8-15 and jot down three thoughts or questions that stand out to you. (There are no right or wrong answers here; you can be as general or specific as you'd like.)

1.

2.

3.

Your responses might be totally different from mine, and that is okay! Here are a few of my thoughts:

- Paul mentions the good news in both verse 9 and verse 15, giving a sense of its priority for the letter.
- The faith of the Roman church was being talked about all over the world. Wow! What would it be like if our faith had that kind of impact today?
- Paul's prayer life, heart to serve, and intensity to spread the good news both convicts and inspires me.
- Paul wanted to encourage others but also recognized his own need to be encouraged. I want to admit my own spiritual needs more readily.

Okay, so I broke the rules and wrote four instead of three. So many rich truths are packed into these verses!

Take a few moments and reflect on how these verses impact you personally. Ask the Lord what truths from Paul's words you most need to hear right now and what action steps you can take in response. Write them below:

Now we are going to camp out on our memory verse for the week. Believe me, these are worth committing to memory!

Take a moment to write Romans 1:16-17 in your own words below:

We find good news in the fact that we can't earn God's love. He makes us right in His sight through faith alone. Theologians refer to this as *justification*. People often explain this word by suggesting we think of it as "just as if I'd never sinned." I like that, don't you? Paul uses judicial terms claiming that we are declared innocent even though we committed the crime of sin because justice was satisfied through Christ.

Let's take a moment to define the words *faith* and *power* found in these verses.

Faith is the Greek word *pistis*.[8] Read the Extra Insight for a biblical definition of faith based on Hebrews 11:1, and then define faith in your own words below:

Extra Insight

Faith shows the reality of what we hope for; it is the evidence of things we cannot see.

(Hebrews 11:1)

How do you want to grow in faith over the course of this study? Write any thoughts that come to mind below:

The Greek word for *power* is *dunamis*.[9] What English word do you think might be derived from this word (what sounds similar)?

The English derivative is *dynamite*. Dynamite has sheer power to change a landscape. In the same way, the good news about Christ has the power to change the landscape of your life. It can transform your thinking, attitudes, and perspective. It can change our circumstances at times, but we can be sure it most definitely will change us.

Have you experienced God's life-changing power in your life recently or in the past? If so, write briefly about it here:

The good news about Christ has the power to change the landscape of your life.

Whether or not you have seen the "dynamite" power of the good news of Jesus recently in your life, how would you like to see His power working in your life in the days and weeks ahead? Here are a few ideas to get you thinking, but don't limit yourself to these. Is there...

- a sin you'd like to overcome?
- a new thought pattern you'd like to embrace?
- a spiritual discipline you'd like to be more consistent in practicing?
- a sense of peace you'd like to maintain in a difficulty?

Write some thoughts below:

The good news about Jesus is powerful. No matter where you may feel powerless today, I pray you will go forward through this day with a great sense of His presence and the same power that can raise the dead to life!

Talk with God

Lord, I need Your power. Help me to see You for who You are. You are all-knowing and all-powerful. Show me the places where I've been trying in my human effort when I need to rest in You. I long to understand and embrace what it means for Your Holy Spirit to be living in me. Help me to hear Your voice today. Amen.

Memory Verse Exercise

Big Idea

Through faith in Christ we receive God's power!

Read the Memory Verse on page 14 several times, and then fill in the blanks below as you recite it:

16 _____ _____ _____ *not* _____ _____ _____
_____ *news* _____ _____. *It is the power of God at work, saving everyone who believes—the Jew first and also the Gentile.* 17 *This Good News tells us how God makes us right in his sight. This is accomplished from start to finish by faith. As the Scriptures say, "It is through faith that a righteous person has life."*

(Romans 1:16-17)

Extra Insight: Important Concepts in Romans

Today we looked at the idea of *justification* in Romans 1:16-17. It's one of several important concepts we will consider in our study. Here's an overview of these terms and their meanings:

Justification—"Justification is a legal matter. God puts the righteousness of Christ on our record in the place of our own sinfulness."[10] Justification is an act, not a process, and no one can change it.

> **Reconciliation**—Reconciliation means "change" or "exchange." "Reconciliation involves a change in the relationship between God and man or man and man. It assumes there has been a breakdown in the relationship, but now there has been a change from a state of enmity and fragmentation to one of harmony and fellowship."[11]

> **Sanctification**—"Sanctification is the process whereby God makes the believer more and more like Christ."[12] Sanctification is not a one-time act but a continual process that may change from day to day.

> **Redemption**—"Finding its context in the social, legal, and religious customs of the ancient world, the metaphor of redemption includes the ideas of loosing from a bond, setting free from captivity or slavery, buying back something lost or sold, exchanging something in one's possession for something possessed by another, and ransoming."[13]

> **Salvation**—"Salvation is a broad concept. It includes the forgiveness of sins, but involves much more, because its basic meaning is soundness or wholeness." It unites justification, reconciliation, sanctification, and redemption together.[14]

DAY 2: THE GREAT EXCHANGE

I remember one of those moments when I needed some reassurance. My circumstances were screaming foul with what I knew to be true about God's promises. Have you ever been there? I asked God if He could send me a tangible reminder that He is real. I remember praying something like, "Could you just write your name in the sky so everyone can have a sign of who you are?" As I sat still for a few moments, I looked up at a beautiful cobalt blue sky full of puffy clouds and laughed at my question. He made that sky, and it screamed of His existence. The words of Psalm 19 invaded my mind:

Scripture Focus

Romans 1:18-32

> *The heavens proclaim the glory of God.*
> *   The skies display his craftsmanship.*
> *Day after day they continue to speak;*
> *   night after night they make him known.*
> *They speak without a sound or word;*
> *   their voice is never heard.*
> *Yet their message has gone throughout the earth,*
> *and their words to all the world.*
>
> *(Psalm 19:1-4a)*

God has written His existence in the sky. What are some glimpses you've seen of God in creation recently?

Read Romans 1:18-20, and note below how God has revealed Himself to the world according to this passage. How are His attributes described?

God's visible creation helps make His invisible qualities known.

We read in these verses that God's visible creation helps make His invisible qualities known. This is called natural revelation. And in verse 18 we read that when we suppress these truths found in the created world, God "shows his anger from heaven." That may conjure up ideas of someone lacking self-control, yet we know the fruit of the Holy Spirit is self-control (Galatians 5:22-23). The Greek word for anger is *orge* and might better be translated "wrath." It is the response of a holy God toward sin (not the sinner) rather than the anger of an emotional person.[15] God's wrath against sin is revealed just as His salvation through Christ is revealed. We can't appreciate the good news of salvation without the bad news about sin.

Read Romans 1:21-25 and answer the following questions:

People knew God, but what two things did they not do in response to their knowledge of God? (v. 21)

What happened to their thinking when they didn't glorify or thank God? (v. 21)

Instead of worshiping God, what did they worship? (v. 23)

What did they trade the truth of God for? (v. 25)

Can you see the progression here?

Knew God but didn't worship or thank Him

Thought up foolish ideas about God

Minds became dark and confused

Claimed to be wise but became fools

Worshiped idols instead of God

God allowed them to follow their own desires

This entire picture can be described as a great exchange—the truth about God for a lie. It starts in the mind and culminates in actions. Specifically, we see idolatry and sexual sin presented here.

How have you seen the progression that leads to this great exchange of truth for a lie played out in the world? You may give a general answer or a specific example.

Now let's bring this a little closer to home as we look at our own minds and hearts.

Read Romans 12:2 in the margin, and write below how we can keep from being conformed to this world:

Do not be conformed to this world, but be transformed by the renewal of your mind, that by testing you may discern what is the will of God, what is good and acceptable and perfect.

Romans 12:2 (ESV)

Our thought lives are secret places. It is here where we alone process the world around us and the feelings inside us. This includes our fantasies, judgments, worries, and self-talk. In our minds we make excuses, justify ourselves, and begin to suppress truth if we aren't careful. If we long to be transformed in our actions, it must start with the renewing of our minds. Sin affects our thinking before it affects our attachments and actions.

What is going on in your secret place lately? When it comes to your thought life, how can you relate personally to the progression we see in these verses? We all exchange God's truth for lies at times, so we need to ask the Holy Spirit

to help us see our blind spots before they lead us down dangerous paths. Active sins often begin with small, subtle thoughts that progress to actions when left unchecked.

Take a moment to write a prayer below asking the Lord to reveal any area of your life where you might be suppressing God's truth:

We read in Romans 1:24 that God handed them over to their own sinful desires. We will find the same Greek verb, *paradidomi*, in verses 26 and 28, which means "to give into the hands (of another)" or "to give over into (one's) power or use."[16] Different Bible versions translate it different ways:

- "Gave them up" (ESV, KJV, NKJV)
- "Gave them over" (NASB, NIV)
- "Abandoned them" (NLT)

Take another look at Romans 1:24-25. How do you interpret what it means to say that God "gives over" or "abandons" people in response to them exchanging truth for a lie?

The whole of Scripture shows a God who is loving and holy.

The whole of Scripture shows a God who is loving and holy. He offered up His only Son as payment for the sin of the world in order to make a way to restore our relationship with Him. This is the great exchange that comes to my mind when I think about God. He exchanged His Son to redeem us. I must admit that the idea of a God who abandons His creatures when they get off track causes me to pause and ask questions—as it should, because God doesn't abandon us when we mess up. These verses have a different meaning. It helps me think of it in terms of a good and loving parent.

When a child is disobedient, a loving parent never stops loving the child or desiring a relationship with the child. But if the child refuses that relationship, choosing to disobey and ignore the parent, then the parent must practice tough love, "abandoning" the child to the consequences of his or her choices. The same is true of God when we refuse His loving correction.

Scripture shows us that God's holy nature demands that He react to sin (see Isaiah 57:15, Proverbs 8:13, 2 Corinthians 7:1, 1 Thessalonians 4:7). If we aren't careful, we can warp our understanding of the Christian faith when we fail to

understand God's holiness and hatred of sin.[17] In a culture that downplays sin and seems to glorify the acceptance of all behavior, I find my own soul forgetting about God's hatred of sin. Yet the Scriptures also tell us of the patience and mercy of God (see Exodus 34:6; Psalm 145:8; Micah 7:19; Romans 2:4; 2 Peter 3:9). So what I see in these verses is a God who loves us and offers Himself but doesn't force Himself on us. If we consistently rebel against His way, He allows us to go down that course even though He sent His Word, prophets, and even His own Son to show us a better way.

As we read the last part of Romans 1, I invite us to have soft hearts. Rather than judging others, let's ask ourselves, "Lord, where have I sinned against you? How can I turn from my sin and follow you with a whole heart in light of all you have done in forgiving me through the blood of your Son?" Let's take the posture of King David, who said, "Search me, O God, and know my heart; / test me and know my anxious thoughts. / Point out anything in me that offends you, / and lead me along the path of everlasting life" (Psalm 139:23-24).

Read Romans 1:26-31, and then write verse 32 below:

God says that sin is serious, yet we do it anyway. It says even worse than sinning is encouraging others to sin. This last verse puts us in a position where we desperately need the help of the Holy Spirit.

What are some ways that we might encourage those who sin—whether knowingly or unknowingly?

I wonder if sometimes our bad example, our ignorance, and either our silence or our verbosity can be a disservice to those around us. At the same time we must guard vigilantly against judgment, self-righteousness, and pride, knowing that we all struggle against sin. Don't you just want to be done with sin?

During a recent move, I ran across some of my college journals. As I read through my prayers written over twenty-five years ago, I was a little discouraged that I still struggle with some of the same issues I was praying about back then. Selfishness, laziness, lack of self-control, and prayerlessness have been persistent issues in my life. I see some growth for sure, but the battle against sin is never-ending. The moment I think I've conquered some area of life, I become prideful about it; and that can lead to . . . sin!

Would you take a moment to be honest about some of the perennial battles with sin you face? Write a few of them below in admission that you struggle against sin like everyone else:

I can't wait until we get to the part in Romans that reminds us one day we will shake off these dying bodies and finally be free from living on a planet cursed by sin. For now, we need God's wisdom. Let's remember that He is serious about sin and wants us to turn from it—not willfully partake in it and encourage others to do the same.

As we end, let's review the three major concepts we covered today.

Check the concept that resonates with you most strongly, and contemplate the questions that follow it. Make notes in the margin if you want.

__ God's natural revelation in creation (Could the Lord be calling you to get out in nature more often and appreciate His handiwork and glorify Him? How could you practically implement this in your daily/weekly routine?)

__ The renewing of your mind (What have you been thinking about most lately? What are some ways you could be more intentional with your thought life?)

__ Your sin habits (Where may you be exchanging God's truth for a lie when it comes to your behavior? How can you rediscover in your mind and heart God's holiness?)

We are only in Day 2 of our study and already we're mining some deep and rich truths. As you begin to apply them in your life and see their value, I hope you'll be even more motivated to continue our exploration of Paul's Letter to the Romans.

Talk with God

Lord, I need You. Break the power of sin in my life. Give me victory as I seek to turn from my sins and turn toward You. Help me to hate sin the way You do, remembering that You always love me. If You tell me something isn't good for me, give me the grace to believe You and accept Your way. Amen.

Memory Verse Exercise

Read the Memory Verse on page 14 several times, and then fill in the blanks below as you recite it:

16 _____ _____ _____ _____ _____ _____

_____ _____ _____ _____ _____. _____ _____

_____ _____ ___ *God* _____ _____, _____

_____ _____ _____—_____ *Jew* _____ _____

_____ _____ _____. [17]*This Good News tells us how God makes us*
right in his sight. This is accomplished from start to finish by faith. As
the Scriptures say, "It is through faith that a righteous person has life."

(Romans 1:16-17)

DAY 3: THE SECRET LIFE

This season in my life has been filled with watching high school football games under Friday night lights. I love being in the stadium, people-watching, and of course cheering for our home team. I notice an "us" against "them" construct at a sporting event. We want to win, and the other team is the enemy. However, we have to be careful of not carrying this kind of thinking out of the stadium and into other areas of life. We can find ourselves labeling people according to generational, political, moral, socioeconomic, or even religious categories, which tends to cause us to make judgments and set ourselves apart as right. I can even find myself doing this as I'm studying Romans, labeling the people in biblical times as "them" and the modern church as "us" and forgetting that we have similar struggles and victories.

Can you think of some "us" against "them" divides that you have witnessed in conversations, on social media, or through movies or television? List one or two labels that come to mind below:

We have different approaches to many things in life, but we must guard against overfocusing on distinctives rather than commonalities. While we can

Big Idea

God reveals Himself through creation and invites us to follow His way rather than give in to sinful desires.

Scripture Focus

Romans 2:1-16

Extra Insight

Paul's references to Jews are directed to the descendants of Israel. The patriarch Jacob's name was changed to Israel by the Lord, and his twelve sons were the ancestors of the twelve tribes of Israel. *Gentile* is the term used of anyone who was not a Jew by birth.

acknowledge our different choices or backgrounds, we need to be careful about writing a narrative of all people who worship, vote, or parent a certain way. We'll see Paul recognizing the "us" against "them" construct today in Romans 2, and we will need a little background information to help us understand the tone and direction of this segment of his letter.

The Roman church was made up of both Jews and Gentiles. Roman Emperor Claudius expelled all of the Jews from Rome in AD 49.[18] This would have caused an exodus of 40,000-50,000 people of Jewish descent, including Jews who converted to Christianity.[19] Six years later Claudius died, and his edict was lifted by his successor Nero, allowing Jews to return to Rome in AD 54.[20] Paul's letter was likely written not long after the return of the Jews to Gentile churches. He wanted to draw them toward one another, which makes sense as we understand they were coming together after a separation that affected leadership responsibilities and church culture. You can imagine how this infected the church with "us" against "them" thinking that needed to be dispelled. Paul is the Jewish apostle to the Gentiles, so he is able to offer instruction while holding clout with both the Jews and the Gentiles.

Keep these historical facts in mind as we discover several key themes today regarding sin, judgment, and favoritism. These are inner life issues that take place in the hearts and minds of all people—those in Paul's day as well as in ours. God addresses these areas because they are the birthplace for attitudes and actions.

Read Romans 2:1-4 below and circle the pronouns you find:

> ¹You may think you can condemn such people, but you are just as bad, and you have no excuse! When you say they are wicked and should be punished, you are condemning yourself, for you who judge others do these very same things. ²And we know that God, in his justice, will punish anyone who does such things. ³Since you judge others for doing these things, why do you think you can avoid God's judgment when you do the same things? ⁴Don't you see how wonderfully kind, tolerant, and patient God is with you? Does this mean nothing to you? Can't you see that his kindness is intended to turn you from your sin?

Did you happen to notice that there is a change from "they" and "them" in chapter 1 to "you" in these verses? As we saw in yesterday's lesson, Paul talked in chapter 1 about people who had abandoned God. He then encouraged the church at Rome to stop pointing out the sins of others and take a hard look at themselves.

Look again at verse 4. What did Paul say is intended to turn them from their sin?

Paul had been preaching the gospel for at least twenty-two years, so he had grown to anticipate the people's tendency to self-righteously think of others with worse sins rather than consider their own.[21] I wonder if you can relate. When you hear sermons, read Scripture, or attend a conference or retreat, do you ever think "so and so needs to hear this part"? (Like maybe your friend or husband or someone whose relation to you ends in "in-law"?) We all have a tendency to focus on those who, in our minds, are "worse" than we are. This keeps us from addressing our own sin issues. Paul points out that God's kindness is meant to cause us to repent, not to take advantage of His grace. This will be an important posture for us as we study Romans. As we study, let's commit now to attempt as best we can to look and listen for ways that we can change personally rather than think of others who need to change.

Write a sentence of intent below stating your desire to respond to God's kindness rather than condemn others as we study:

This next section may seem to fly in the face of Paul's good news that God makes us right in His sight by faith alone. But let's not forget that the title of this week's study is "Good News About Faith"!

Read Romans 2:5-11, and write below any questions or comments that come to mind:

The first question that comes to mind for me is, "Is salvation a result of a person's good works or by faith alone?" How would you answer if someone asked you this question?

I hope after reviewing our memory verse for the past two days, you will recall that Romans tells us that salvation is accomplished from start to finish

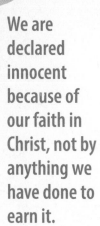

We are declared innocent because of our faith in Christ, not by anything we have done to earn it.

8God saved you by his grace when you believed. And you can't take credit for this; it is a gift from God. 9Salvation is not a reward for the good things we have done, so none of us can boast about it. 10For we are God's masterpiece. He has created us anew in Christ Jesus, so we can do the good things he planned for us long ago.
(Ephesians 2:8-10)

by faith. So how are we to understand verse 6 that says, "He will judge everyone according to what they have done"?

I have read many commentators' opinions on how to understand this verse and others like it. What we must remember is that we will be judged by our works. All of us will be found guilty since none of us lives and acts in full accordance with God's law except for Christ. So we will be judged by what we have done, and all of humanity will fail that standard. But that is what makes the good news so good! Christ came and died for us to pay the penalty of our sin and save us from death and destruction. We are declared innocent because of our faith in Christ, not by anything we have done to earn it.

Of course, this doesn't mean we shouldn't do good things.

Read Ephesians 2:8-10 in the margin. Why are we created anew in Christ Jesus?

Which comes first—our salvation or our good works?

The only way we can escape judgment from sin and have the power to do good in life is through faith alone. When we believe God's Word and turn away from our sin in faith, the outworking of that in our life will result in doing good works. The order is crucial here!

It's not…Do good works ⟶ then God will save us.

Rather, it's…Believe God's good news by faith ⟶ which results in good works.

In the midst of Paul's letter to the Roman Christians with its emphasis on doctrine or belief, we don't want to lose sight of the grace of God. As we try to balance God's justice and mercy, we must remember that mercy triumphs over judgment (James 2:13). We must always look for God's heart and not get tripped up on isolated phrases.

Now read Romans 2:12-15, and label each statement with a "J" if it pertains to the Jews or a "G" if it pertains to the Gentiles:

_____ **1. When they sin, they will be destroyed even though they never had God's written law. (v. 12)**

_____ 2. They have God's law and will be judged by it when they don't obey it. (v. 12)

_____ 3. They don't have God's written law, but they prove they know it by obeying it. (v. 14)

_____ 4. God's law is written on their hearts, and their conscience either condemns them or tells them they are doing right. (v. 15)

Why do you think Paul distinguishes between Jews and Gentiles so much in this chapter?

Paul is trying to bring both groups together and help them see that God truly doesn't practice favoritism. He wants them to remember that they are all equal—in consequences of sin and judgment and in grace through faith.

What would you identify as Paul's main message from Romans 2:1-15?

Now read Romans 2:16 and paraphrase it below:

Paul seems to sum up his message succinctly in this verse. He clearly states that everyone is going to be judged, and no one is able to do enough to warrant salvation. We all must humbly come to God in faith, confessing our need for Him and our inability to be good enough in our human strength. Paul is under-cutting those who depend on their limited obedience to the law for salvation. He wants the Roman church to get away from the Jew versus Gentile categories as an "us" against "them" construct. He wants them to see each other as people who recognize their need for God and turn to Him in faith—no longer seeking to live for themselves but coming together in pursuit of God.

Answers: 1. G 2. J 3. G 4. G

How can we in the church today acknowledge distinctions while still focusing on commonalities?

God made us unique with different personality types, backgrounds, and gifts. We should celebrate our differences without mentally categorizing people with an "us" against "them" construct. It is often in our thoughts and heart attitudes that favoritism takes place. That is the place where Christ looks, so we must evaluate our secret lives.

Take some time to reflect on your private thought life. Where has favoritism, judgment, or shame crept in? Write a brief prayer below inviting God into the secret places of your heart and mind:

Remember, it is God's kindness that leads us to repentance. Don't let these verses about judgment bring any shame! They are meant to convict us but never condemn us (Romans 8:1). May we all focus on the Lord's patience and kindness as we seek to grow deeper in our faith through our study of Romans.

Talk with God

Lord, I need You desperately. Help me to lay down my microscope and pick up my mirror. Change me in my secret places so I can love and serve from a place of humility and authenticity. Amen.

Memory Verse Exercise

Read the Memory Verse on page 14 several times, and then fill in the blanks below as you recite it:

16 _____ _____ _____ _____ _____ _____

_____ _____ _____ _____ _____. ____ ____

____ _____ __ *God* ____ _____, _____

_____ ____ _____—____ *Jew* _____ ____

____ ____ _____. [17]*This* _____ ____ ____ ____ ____

____ _____ ___ *right* ____ ____ *sight. This is accomplished*

from start to finish by faith. As the Scriptures say, "It is through faith that a righteous person has life."

(Romans 1:16-17)

DAY 4: A CHANGED HEART

What kind of gear, gadgets, or stuff do you tend to gather? Is it sports equipment, clothing, or home decor? Clutter is my enemy, and I like to keep things pretty simple. Someone recently described my decorating style as "sparse." I'm not sure if that was a compliment, but I'll own it. I mean, I love a delivery box at my door like the next girl, but mine are usually filled with household items or commentaries. Then it hit me: if I collect anything, it is commentaries. Right now I'm staring at a stack of them, and it makes me happy just to be near the words written by great theologians of the past and present.

Okay, it's your turn. What is something you collect, or what paraphernalia for a hobby or interest do you get giddy to purchase?

Where am I going with all this talk about stuff? Today we will delve into Paul's teaching that gets at the heart of our faith. He helps us see that we can overfocus on the stuff of our spirituality to the point that we miss the heart of it. It would be like a runner who got so excited about his or her specialized watch, shoes, or fanny pack that the actual running became ancillary to the gear. This can happen to the best of us. It certainly happened to some of the Jews who got caught up in the laws and rituals and lost sight of the God behind it all. This would be tantamount to us worshiping the Bible rather than the God who inspired it.

As we study today, we are going to focus on three key statements: 1) Take a Look (2:17-24), 2) Give Up (2:25-29), and 3) Get Real (3:1-8). Let's get started!

Take a Look

Before we read Romans 2:17-24, I want to help you understand something about Paul's style. He is using an ancient debating technique known as diatribe in which "the proponent of a position anticipated opponents' criticisms by raising those points before they did."[22] You'll see Paul's use of irony and argument as he seems to know what the audience might be thinking as he is writing.

Go ahead and read Romans 2:17-24, and write below how the Jews Paul was writing to saw themselves (vv. 17-20):

Now list what Paul accused them of doing in verses 21-24:

What irony is highlighted in verse 23?

Paul seems to be saying, "Take a look in the mirror of God's law and see yourselves. You are boasting, but you've failed to see your own sins because of your pride and condemnation of others." In verse 24 Paul refers to Isaiah 52:5 where the prophet speaks of deliverance. They were headed into exile to Assyria because they failed to show the surrounding nations God's nature. Instead the people around them blasphemed God because of their poor example. They needed to take a look and grow in self-awareness. Here Paul hits right at the heart of the disconnection between what we teach and how we live.

God's Word is a mirror. We need to regularly "take a look" so we can see clearly where we need to realign with God's heart and mission. We don't want to get so caught up with the letter of His Words that we miss the spirit of them. We would never want those around us to be turned off to our God because of our lack of self-awareness. God has called us to be a light to those around us just as He entrusted the Jews with His message.

Take a few minutes now to "take a look" in the mirror of God's Word. Ask God to reveal any areas where your profession and your practice are inconsistent. Jot a few notes below regarding places where you need to take a closer look to see yourself more accurately:

Give Up

My tendency after I have taken a look and seen the incongruity in my prayer life, the way I treat my family, or my attitude toward poverty is to start working a plan to fix it. (Anybody with me?) But the next section of Scripture reminds us that rather than trying to work this out in our own strength, God calls us to give up. Yep, you read that right.

Read Romans 2:25-29 and write below how God defines a true Jew:

Paul didn't launch into a diatribe style here, talking about working harder at serving God in anticipation of potential questions or objections. Instead he tells them that the only way to God is a change of heart that is produced by the Spirit. If the law was a major distinctive of the Jews, then circumcision was a close second; and many had placed unwarranted confidence in this practice.

What are some Christian practices or traditions that people sometimes elevate above the heart behind it?

Our traditions and ordinances are beautiful things meant to point us to spiritual truths. Communion, baptism, praise music, Bible translations, or even the crosses used to adorn our churches can be twisted into pride issues that cause us to war with each other rather than point to Christ.

This is why, after taking a look, we need to give up. We give up on our efforts to be righteous apart from faith. We give up trusting in the sacraments, practices, people, buildings, or ministries that surround our faith, putting our trust in Christ alone. This is the good news about faith. We don't just start with faith and then work at living for God with effort.

Is there an area where you have been trying to follow God in your own strength? Where is the Lord calling you to give up? Write a prayer below admitting your need and asking the Holy Spirit to change your heart in that area:

Get Real

So we have learned that God's law is a mirror and we need to take a look. It also reminds us that we can't fulfill its requirements by pulling ourselves up by our bootstraps and trying harder. Now let's discover how God's law calls us to get real!

Extra Insight

Circumcision is the removal of the foreskin of a male child, which happened eight days after birth in Jewish culture. It was a sign that the whole nation was dedicated to God (Genesis 17:10).

The only way to God is a change of heart that is produced by the Spirit.

Extra Insight

Theologians came up with a term to describe how the Jews entered their covenant with God by faith and then tried to stay in the covenant by obeying the law. It is called covenantal nomism.[23]

Read Romans 3:1-8 and write below what is revealed about God's character:

Paul used a verse from the Hebrew Scriptures to substantiate his point. At the end of verse 4 Paul quotes Psalm 51:4. David wrote this psalm after he was confronted about his adultery with Bathsheba and the murder of her husband, and he was agreeing that God's judgment was right. Paul is showing that God remains faithful even when humans are not.

God is faithful and true. His law was never intended to save but to reveal our inability to fulfill it. When we discover the futility of our attempts at obedience to the law, it brings us to God, aware of our need to believe Him by faith. But here is another point where Paul headed the reader off at the pass. Using the logic that our unfaithfulness points to God's grace, he knew objections would surface saying that we should sin more to highlight God's grace. In Romans 6:1-2 he laid it out even more clearly: "Well then, should we keep on sinning so that God can show us more and more of his wonderful grace? Of course not! Since we have died to sin, how can we continue to live in it?" Another parental metaphor may be helpful here.

Even if you aren't a parent, imagine someone you love is in your care. You don't want this person to obey and make wise choices to earn your love. You already love her or him to pieces. What, then, would your motive be for wanting your loved one to do right things?

As a parent, I greatly desire for my children to choose wisely because I love them. I know that God's way leads to life and sin brings suffering. God loves us, and He has connected faith and faithfulness. When people believe God from a place of authenticity, positive changes happen that lead to life. Out of a transformed heart comes a transformed life.

God used the law to help His people get real about their lives. He wants us to get real about ours too.

Turn back to Romans 2:29, and write below one of the marks of a person with a changed heart:

Any other people pleasers out there? God says one of the ways we can test the state of things in our hearts is to look at where we seek praise. As we get real with the Lord, we discover that He is truly our audience of One.

Take a moment to record below any truths that stood out to you from our three areas of study today:

Take a Look:

Give Up:

Get Real:

Like those Paul is addressing in these verses, we have similar tendencies toward turning toward symbols, practices, and human effort to prop ourselves up. We have to constantly evaluate where the affections of our hearts lie. My prayer today is that as we grow in faith, we will grow in faithfulness.

Talk with God

Lord, I want to understand the way You are calling me to take a look and see myself from Your perspective. Show me where I need to give up striving and turn toward You. Help me to get real about who You are. You are the truth, and You are always faithful. I want to be like You and to seek approval from You rather than look for validation in the eyes of people. Thank You for the good news about faith today! Amen.

Memory Verse Exercise

Read the Memory Verse on page 14 several times, and then fill in the blanks below as you recite it:

16_____ ____ _____ ____ _____ ____
_____ _____ _____ _____ _____. ___ ___
____ _____ __ *God* ____ _____, _____
_____ ___ _____— ___ *Jew* _____ ___
___ ___ _____. 17*This* _____ ___ ____

Big Idea

God's law helps us take a look, give up, and get real as we seek to understand the good news about faith.

_____ _____ _____ _____ *right* _____ _____ *sight. This* _____

_____ _____ _____ *to* _____ _____ _____.

As the Scriptures say, "It is through faith that a righteous person has
life."

(Romans 1:16-17)

DAY 5: BAD NEWS
AND GOOD NEWS

**Scripture
Focus**

Romans 3:9-31

Has anyone ever asked you if you want the good news or the bad news first?
My husband loves to start conversations that way. I always want the bad news
first. I want to get the dread out of the way so I can fully appreciate whatever the
good news might be. Paul operated in the same way when it came to the good
and bad news. He starts with the bad stuff. In order for us to appreciate this good
news about Christ, we first have to understand the bad news about sin. Paul
has taken the time to be sure the Roman church doesn't trust in themselves—
either in their heritage as Jews or in their lack of the law as Gentiles—as a way
to excuse their depravity. He wants them to understand they are all on a level
playing field when it comes to sin problems. No one has an edge over another.
Basically, we are all a hot mess.

**Read Romans 3:9-20 and summarize the point Paul wants to drive
home in one sentence:**

Sin entered the world when our great-great-great-(and a whole bunch of
other "greats") grandparents Adam and Eve chose to give in to temptation
and disobey God's instructions. They passed down the tendency toward sin
so that now everyone is born knowing instinctively how to do it. We all battle
the flesh or sin nature, and the law reveals our inability to live according to
God's instructions. Praise God that through Christ we can experience victory
and obedience to God!

Once again Paul turns to the Hebrew Scriptures to prove his point about
sin.

**Read the following passages and underline any phrases or statements
that correspond with the verses we just read from Romans 3:**

¹*Only fools say in their hearts,*
   "There is no God."
They are corrupt, and their actions are evil;
   not one of them does good!

²*The Lord looks down from heaven*
   on the entire human race;
he looks to see if anyone is truly wise,
   if anyone seeks God.
³*But no, all have turned away;*
   all have become corrupt.
No one does good,
   not a single one!"

                    (Psalm 14:1-3)

Their tongues sting like a snake;
   the venom of a viper drips from their lips.

                    (Psalm 140:3)

Their mouths are full of cursing, lies, and threats.
   Trouble and evil are on the tips of their tongues.

                    (Psalm 10:7)

Their feet run to do evil,
   and they rush to commit murder.
They think only about sinning.
   Misery and destruction always follow them.
They don't know where to find peace
   or what it means to be just and good.
They have mapped out crooked roads,
   and no one who follows them knows a moment's peace.

                    (Isaiah 59:7-8)

Paul didn't come up with his illustrations for sin on his own. He drew them right out of the Hebrew Scriptures. Did you notice the references to body parts in these passages? Sin is associated with the tongue, mouth, heart, and even feet.

Extra Insight

Paul was a Jewish scholar who studied under a prestigious rabbi named Gamaliel before he met Christ on the Damascus road. His breadth of understanding in the Scriptures helps him speak with authority.

What is your reaction to the strong language used here regarding sin? Write any thoughts or questions that come to mind from these verses:

Okay, we have waded through the bad news pretty thoroughly. What we find is that because sin entered the world through the choice of Adam and Eve, we are prone to sin. Our problem is not just a knowledge issue, or Jesus could have come and given us more knowledge. Only a Savior paying the penalty can free us from sin. If there was another way, why would God sacrifice his own Son? The sacrificial system of the Israelites reveals that only a perfect blood sacrifice could atone for sin (Leviticus 17:11; Hebrews 9:22). Jesus Himself said that He is the way, the truth, and the life and that no one can come to the Father except through Him (John 14:6).

So, sin is the bad news. It's important to temper this message about sin with the recognition that we are made in God's image and have great value as His beloved creation. That's why He sent His Son to save us from sin. So although the bad news of sin can be discouraging, it brings us to God and some very good news!

Let's camp for the rest of the day on the good news.

Read Romans 3:21-31 and write below how you would explain the message found in these verses to a person who had never heard it before:

I remember sharing this message with a neighbor sitting in a restaurant. Her daughter had attended a backyard Bible club at our home and had responded to this message in faith. I felt the Holy Spirit nudging me to explain what had been taught to her daughter and how she had responded. When I told my neighbor about everyone being a sinner and faith in Christ being the only way to God, she said this: "So you are saying that I could be a good person my whole life and try to do what's right and not believe in God, and some rapist or murderer could choose to believe in Christ by faith and he would go to heaven and I wouldn't."

Ouch. How would you have answered that?

I said this, "My understanding of what God says in His Word is that forgiven people go to heaven rather than good people. How would you know when you have been good enough?" My friend thought that all sounded pretty crazy to her.

However, later that year after we had more conversations and she read a book I shared with her, she told me that this faith stuff was beginning to make more sense to her.

I share this to say that I realize these words may not sound like good news to everyone—at least not at first. If that's you, I want to encourage you to hang in there through our study of Romans. Keep asking questions, being honest, and seeking God. He can handle every doubt or hang-up we have.

Romans 3:23 reminds us that we all fall short of God's glorious standard apart from Christ. If we were all standing at the edge of the Grand Canyon trying to throw our "goodness" rock to reach the other side, we all would fail to get it across. There are some really amazing people who have lived incredible lives for God. I'm thinking Mother Teresa could hurl her "goodness" rock a pretty good distance. But no one could make it all the way to the other side. The chasm is too great. But in Christ, our faith is enough!

Paul wanted the Romans to be clear on what God had done and how it impacted their lives in every way. *It is the good news that changes everything.* Christ's death and resurrection bridges the gap between a Holy God and sinful people. He even helped them understand how those who lived before Christ were affected by this good news.

What do we learn in Romans 3:25-26 about those who lived in the past?

The old covenant wasn't a mistake that God scrapped when it didn't seem to work out. From the start, the first covenant foreshadowed and pointed to Christ. Before the promised Messiah, the Christ, stepped out of eternity and into time, men and women believed by faith in His coming, and righteousness was credited to them.

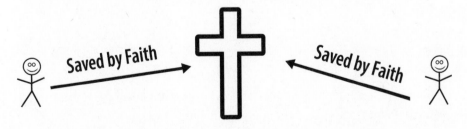

We have the benefit of hindsight to believe with even more knowledge and understanding of the promised Messiah. In this passage Paul used metaphors germane to the original audience such as the courts, commerce, and religious system:

Courts: In Romans 3:24, Paul used judicial language in saying that we are "declared" righteous, which is referred to as justification. The penalty of sin had been taken away.[24]

Commerce: When he speaks of redemption in Romans 3:24 it means "'to liberate by paying a price.' . . . In Paul's day the [word] referred to the way in which people could pay money to buy the freedom of slaves or prisoners of war."[25]

Religious System: In Romans 3:25 Paul also uses a religious term, *propitiation*, referring to the cover of the Ark of the Covenant in the temple.[26] The readers of this letter would have associated the word *propitiation* with the sacrificial system where the blood of an animal represented the cleansing of sin through blood. These sacrifices were shadows that hinted at the sacrifice of Christ.

Let these metaphors sink in as you think of your own life. Even if you are not feeling innocent, free, and worthy today, God says you are. Take a moment to write your name in the blanks below:

_____ has been declared righteous even though

_____ has done wrong.

_____ is freed from slavery to sin.

God's wrath is satisfied through the blood of Christ so

_____ can freely enter the most holy place to spend eternity with God.

Write a brief prayer of response to the above statements asking the Lord to help you see yourself the way He sees you:

When we live in the light of God's love for us, our faith spurs us on to love freely.

When we live in the light of God's love for us, our faith spurs us on to love freely. God's message to us in Romans 1–3 is not:

- Try harder.
- Work more.
- Earn your way.
- Clean yourself up.

It is two simple words: *Have faith.*

So this is where we start—believing that we all fall short of God's glorious standard and need a Savior. We believe that Christ died for our sins. By faith we come to God and choose to follow Him. Perhaps this is the first time you are hearing this good news. If so, that is amazing, and I pray these truths will continue to soak in as we continue our study in Romans. Or perhaps you've heard this good news before—maybe for years; maybe even as long as you can remember. Our journeys of faith may look very different, but the object of them is the same. Our faith is in Christ alone.

Talk with God

Lord, I need You. Thank You so much for the cross where Jesus was the ultimate sacrifice for sin and declared us righteous. Thank You for this good news about faith. Help me to stop doing and start being who You say that I am. Amen.

Memory Verse Exercise

Read the Memory Verse on page 14 several times, and then fill in the blanks below as you recite it:

16 _____ _____ _____ _____ _____
_____ _____ _____ _____ _____. ____ ____
____ _____ ___ God ____ _____, _____
_____ ____ _____ —____ Jew _____
____ ___ ____ _____. ¹⁷This _____ ____ ____
____ _____ _____ ____ right ____ ____ sight. This
____ _____ ____ _____ ____ _____
_____. As ____ _____ ____, " ____ ____
_____ ____ ____ __ _____ _____
____ _____."

(Romans 1:16-17)

Big Idea sidebar

Big Idea

While we find bad news in sin's power to separate us from God, we rejoice that Christ died to satisfy the penalty of sin and bring us back into fellowship with God.

Weekly Wrap Up

Review the Big Idea for each day, and then write any personal application that comes to mind.

Day 1: The Power
Big Idea: Through faith in Christ we receive God's power!

Personal Application:_____
_____

Day 2: The Great Exchange
Big Idea: God reveals Himself through creation and invites us to follow His way rather than give in to sinful desires.

Personal Application:_____

_____

Day 3: The Secret Life
Big Idea: In the secret places of our hearts and minds we invite Christ to help us view others, ourselves, and God correctly.

Personal Application:_____

_____

Day 4: A Changed Heart
Big Idea: God's law helps us to take a look, give up, and get real as we seek to understand the good news about faith.

Personal Application:_____

_____

Day 5: Bad News and Good News
Big Idea: While we find bad news in sin's power to separate us from God, we rejoice that Christ died to satisfy the penalty of sin and bring us back into fellowship with God.

Personal Application:_____

_____

VIDEO VIEWER GUIDE: WEEK 1

GOOD NEWS ABOUT FAITH

The good news about faith isn't about _____ but about

_____.

Romans 1:3-4

Romans 1:16-17

God hates sin because it can't be _____ and brings

_____.

Romans 1:21-22, 25

Romans 2:1-3

God's _____ leads us to turn from our sin.

Romans 2:4

Week 2

Good News About Hope

Romans 4–5

Memory Verse

But God demonstrates his own love for us in this: While we were still sinners, Christ died for us.

(Romans 5:8 NIV)

DAY 1: HOPE IN A FAMILY

When I was in elementary school, we sang a song at church that went something like this:

> Father Abraham had many sons
> Many sons had Father Abraham.
> I am one of them, and so are you.
> So let's all praise the Lord.

Then as we sang, we would shake our right arm, and then our left. We moved on to shaking our legs, turning around, and eventually sitting down in exhaustion and laughter. I never thought much about the words back then. It was just a fun song with lots of actions. But it has come to mind several times as I've been studying Romans 4 where Paul explains what it means to be a part of Abraham's spiritual family.

This week we are celebrating the good news about hope in Romans 4 and 5. To understand this hope, we have to get back to our roots. I wish I had some Jewish ancestry in my bloodline, but a recent DNA test showed that I am less than 1 percent Jewish. However, I can sing "Father Abraham" with great confidence that I am "one of them" because of what we learn in Romans 4. We may not be related genetically, but spiritually I can claim Abraham as father; and if you are a person who lives by faith in Christ, you can too.

Read Romans 4:1-5. What do these verses tell us that God uses as the basis of whether we are counted as righteous?

Our faith in him

While faith as the basis for salvation may be familiar to us, it was a paradigm shift for many in the original audience of Jews and Gentiles. Most Jews revered Abraham, and some commentators point out that they thought he found favor with God because of his character and conduct.[3] Paul wanted his readers to understand that Abraham didn't have a special relationship with God based on his actions; it was his faith that set him apart. The Lord made promises to Abraham in Genesis 12 that are referred to as the Abrahamic Covenant.

Read the following verses, and underline the various forms of the word *bless* that you find:

Scripture Focus

Romans 4:1-12

Digging Deeper

For a deeper look at the practice of circumcision as a sign and seal, check out the Digging Deeper article for Week 2, "Covenant Signs," (see AbingdonWomen .com/Romans).

Extra Insight

Paul is correcting the prevalent belief of merit theology.[1] He used the Greek banking term *logizomai* in verse 3, which means "to pass to one's account," to express that God "counted" or "reckoned" or "imputed" righteousness to us by faith.[2]

"I will make you into a great nation. I will <u>bless you</u> and make you famous, and you will <u>be a blessing</u> to others. I <u>will bless</u> those who bless you and curse those who treat you with contempt. All the families on earth <u>will be blessed through</u> you."

(Genesis 12:2-3)

Which aspect of this blessing relates to you and me?

> *We are part of all the families on earth*

We are part of the "all families" that will be blessed. Paul helped the Roman church see that they are included in the fulfillment of this promise. Both Jews and Gentiles will be included by faith. Both groups are the children of Abraham and heirs to his promise. Paul wanted the church at Rome to fully understand that this wasn't a "new" plan. It is a fulfillment of the original one. To illustrate that doing good works wasn't what earned God's favor, Paul refers to another figure from the Hebrew Scriptures—included in our Old Testament.

Read Romans 4:6-12 and answer the following questions:

After Abraham, who is Paul's second witness from the Old Testament? (v. 6)

> *David*

In Romans 4:7-8, Paul quotes Psalm 32:1-2, a psalm of David. Do you know what King David had done before he wrote this? (We referred to it last week when looking at another psalm David wrote, Psalm 51.)

Extra Insight

If you would like to read more about David's sin and repentance for greater context, read 2 Samuel 11–12.

David penned those words in Psalm 32 just after confessing that he had committed adultery and murder. David stands as a great example of someone who didn't always obey the law but had a pattern of repenting of sin with a tender heart. He displayed faith by believing God forgave Him. For both Abraham and David, we get a sense of a divine reckoning rather than human effort.[4] It is here we find our identity as God's people. We display our own faith when we refuse to hinge our hope to our human actions, attitudes, or obedience. When we believe God loves us, forgives us, and transforms us, we are living the legacy of great people such as Abraham and David.

Paul taught these rich truths about faith to unify the Roman church, which was divided into Jewish and Gentile factions. He wanted the believers to understand that their faith bound the church together, so he drew them toward one another.

You may or may not be connected to a local church, but let's consider together the importance of faith community.

One commentator made this bold statement: "A churchless Christianity makes about as much sense as a Christless Christianity."[5] Do you agree or disagree, and why?

You need to be connected to other Christians and hear the word or you can't grow

Whether or not we agree to that extreme, we can see that Abraham's story is a foundational narrative in forming our own understanding and worldview. By seeing ourselves as spiritual children of Abraham, we learn that our believing means belonging. We realize that we are part of a large faith family with a long history. We are rooted deeply in something much bigger than our individual lives. We are part of the family of God.

Are you now or have you ever been connected to a larger family of believers? If so, write a few sentences below regarding how being part of a local church body has impacted your faith (either negatively or positively):

Parsonage across street - Church down street - Awana - Youth group - 3 of 5 bridesmaids

When I think about this question, I recall Sunday school teachers who shaped my early views of God as they taught Bible stories each week. In addition to my parents, they were a huge part of my spiritual formation. I reflect on youth group trips when I felt a sense of belonging during awkward years of insecurity. As a young mom, my Bible study ladies helped normalize the difficulties associated with breastfeeding, potty-training, and sleep deprivation; and I found a place to process how parenting impacted my spiritual life. None of these experiences was as idyllic as it sounds on paper. I attended different churches according to where we lived and where my husband pastored through the years, and I learned that every body of believers is imperfect, just as every family is. Church relationships also have brought deep pain in my life during different seasons.

Perhaps you can relate. You even may have experienced spiritual abuse at the hands of church leaders. I've heard someone say there is no pain like church pain. This might be because we expect more from those who claim the name of Christ. In reality, all leaders are flawed and make mistakes. Yet we can't allow past pain to prevent us from belonging to a faith community. What hurts us can be the very thing God uses to heal us. If we've experienced wounds in a church, God may use a church filled with love and grace in a redemptive way.

There are many ways church relationships can parallel family relationships. Families spend time together. They celebrate special events. They mourn together when difficulties arise. They fight and make up. They come together when another person needs help. We can find hope in seeing our local church body as a faith family where we can connect and grow.

> I wonder…is God calling you to get connected with a church if you aren't already? Or could He be asking you to become more committed to your faith family? Put a check beside any suggestions that stand out to you, or write an idea the Holy Spirit may be prompting as a next step in regard to your involvement in a local church:
>
> ___ Begin the process of prayerfully visiting churches.
>
> ___ Prioritize regular attendance of worship services, special events, conferences, and/or retreats.
>
> ___ Commit to serve in an area of ministry at your church (greeters, children or teen ministry, and etc.).
>
> ___ Join or engage more regularly in a small group Bible study where you can develop community.
>
> ___ Other:_____

Extra Insight

In Romans, there are over sixty references to faith or unbelief.[6]

Those who choose to follow Jesus are not meant to live the Christian life in isolation.

Today we've seen that those who choose to follow Jesus are not meant to live the Christian life in isolation. As we allow these truths to sink deep and we pursue greater connection with those in our local church bodies, we can find hope in knowing we are part of a faith family with a rich heritage.

Talk with God

Lord, it is incredible to imagine that when Abraham walked the earth, You had me in mind as someone to bless. Help me to believe Your promises the way Abraham and David did. Show me how my faith family can help me grow in trusting You more, especially when life doesn't seem to match up with what I read in Your Word. I want to do life alongside other believers and show the world what it means to believe and belong. Amen.

Memory Verse Exercise

Read the Memory Verse on page 46 several times, and then fill in the blanks below as you recite it:

But ____Grod____ demonstrates his own love for us in this: While we were still __sinners__, Christ died for _us_.

(Romans 5:8)

DAY 2: AGAINST ALL HOPE

Have you hoped for something recently? My husband and I take very different postures toward hope because of our personality differences. I'm guarded with my hope factor when it comes to most things. I don't want to be so hopeful that I'm unprepared. For example, we lived in the same house for nineteen years and put it up for sale in order to move to a new town. I wanted to crunch numbers in case it took a few months to sell so that we could be prepared financially for double payments. My husband was certain it would sell in a few days. He is usually hopeful and, unfortunately, I tend to plan for the worst for fear of experiencing disappointment. In the end, our house sold more slowly than my husband thought it would but faster than I expected.

Both postures toward hope can have pitfalls. If you are overly optimistic, you might not be prepared. If you don't allow yourself to be hopeful, you can miss blessings and develop a negative bent.

How would you rate your hope level in regard to things you want to happen—whether small things such as hoping for good weather or big things such as hoping to have a child? Put an X on the line for where you generally fall:

Extremely hopeful	Somewhat hopeful	Mildly hopeful	Not very hopeful

————————————X—————————————————————

What is something you are hoping for right now?

Wisdom for 2023

Big Idea

We find hope by being connected to a larger family of faith as children of Abraham.

Scripture Focus

Romans 4:13-25

Extra Insight

"God does keep a record of our good works, so that He might reward us when Jesus comes, but He is not keeping a record of our sins."[7]

Promise, hope, and faith build on each other and intertwine to help us trust God with our lives.

This week we are focusing on the good news about hope. While Paul continues to discuss faith in chapter 4, he introduces its relationship with hope to develop a deeper gospel understanding. We'll break down today's passage using three key words found in the text. *Promise*, *hope*, and *faith* build on each other and intertwine to help us trust God with our lives.

Read Romans 4:13-18 below and answer the questions that follow.

13Clearly, God's promise to give the whole earth to Abraham and his descendants was based not on his obedience to God's law, but on a right relationship with God that comes by faith. 14If God's promise is only for those who obey the law, then faith is not necessary and the promise is pointless. 15For the law always brings punishment on those who try to obey it. (The only way to avoid breaking the law is to have no law to break!)

16So the promise is received by faith. It is given as a free gift. And we are all certain to receive it, whether or not we live according to the law of Moses, if we have faith like Abraham's. For Abraham is the father of all who believe. 17That is what the Scriptures mean when God told him, "I have made you the father of many nations." This happened because Abraham believed in the God who brings the dead back to life and who creates new things out of nothing.

18Even when there was no reason for hope, Abraham kept hoping— believing that he would become the father of many nations. For God had said to him, "That's how many descendants you will have!"

How many times do you find the word *promise* in these verses?

4

What is God's promise to Abraham *not* based on? (v. 13)

his obedience

If God's promise is only for those who obey the law, what does that make the promise? (v. 14)

pointless - no one could do it

How is the promise received? (v. 16)

by faith, freely

What kind of God did Abraham believe in? (v. 17)

One who brings dead back to life

Here we discover the first usage of the word *promise* (*epangelia*) in Romans.[8] Paul is building on what we found in yesterday's lesson—that hope in our spiritual family is tied all the way back to Father Abraham. The importance of the key word *promise* cannot be overstated as it relates to our faith. We live in a culture that often values faith in and of itself, suggesting that where we place our faith matters less than our intensity and passion to believe in something. Yet Paul emphasizes the promises of God that are tied to our faith. Faith alone isn't powerful.

When the Israelites placed their faith in counterfeit gods, they experienced nothing but disappointment. But when our faith is rooted in a true God who loves, intervenes, and has the power to work in our lives, that's where we find hopeful news.

Abraham believed in a God who could raise the dead and bring something out of nothing. His belief wasn't dreamed up or carved out of wood and dressed up like the idols that surrounded him. He believed what God had revealed to him. Even when his reality didn't match his theology and God's promises ran contrary to his logic and feelings, he believed anyway.

What are some of God's promises that you have chosen to stand on even when they haven't "felt" true in your life and circumstances?

That he knows what's best for me
The beatitudes   He will not give me more than I can take

Abraham received God's promises directly from God. We have the Bible, which is filled with God's promises, and we must exercise good judgment as we apply these promises in our lives. Some of them are specific for individuals or groups of people, and others are universal, relating to all people of all time. While we find many promises in Scripture, as one of the gals in the pilot group for this study said, ultimately the promise is a person. Our faith is not in a concept or idea; it is in a person, Jesus—our Savior who came to rescue us from sin and restore our relationship with God. So Jesus fulfilled the promises laced throughout the Old Testament foreshadowing His coming.

In the following verses, underline the words *promise* and *Jesus* as you encounter them:

And it is one of King David's descendants, Jesus, who is God's promised Savior of Israel!

(Acts 13:23)

And this is God's plan: Both Gentiles and Jews who believe the Good News share equally in the riches inherited by God's children. Both are part of the same body, and both enjoy the promise of blessings because they belong to Christ Jesus.

(Ephesians 3:6)

But now Jesus, our High Priest, has been given a ministry that is far superior to the old priesthood, for he is the one who mediates for us a far better covenant with God, based on better promises.

(Hebrews 8:6)

Jesus fulfills the promises of God. In fact, Revelation 19:10b says that the whole point of prophecy is about Jesus: "For the essence of prophecy is to give a clear witness for Jesus." So our faith must be tied to the promise of God, and that promise is Jesus!

Take a moment now to write a brief reflection or prayer thanking God for sending Jesus so that you could have a restored relationship with your Creator:

Thank you God for abundant blessings, the biggest one being Jesus who died for my sins.

How does what we've read about faith and promises relate to this week's theme of hope? To answer that, let's consider that key word *hope*. How would you describe the difference between faith and hope?

Faith, we are certain about Hope is optimism for possibilities

I found that question challenging to answer. Maybe you did too. I always like to go back to the original Greek language that the New Testament was written in to see what the words express. In the Letter to the Romans, the word *faith* is the Greek word *pistis*, which Strong's concordance defines as "conviction of the truth of anything, belief."[9] The word *hope* is the Greek word *elpis*, which Strong's concordance defines as "expectation of good."[10]

As I read these definitions, I see this distinction: *Faith* means I believe something to be true, while *hope* means that I expect it to be good. Many times it takes faith to believe that following God will ultimately lead to good. Jesus

gave His life on the cross, which we know didn't feel good in the moment but led to the reconciliation of God and people—the essence of the good news that changes everything.

Now having defined these words, let's take a look at Abraham's hope.

Read Romans 4:18-19 and describe Abraham's hope below:

He could only dream of possibilities at such an age

Abraham had no reason to expect something good. From a human perspective, the promise that his wife, Sarah, would have a child when she was past the age of childbearing seems impossible. It wasn't that Abraham blindly ignored biological facts; he just chose to believe in supernatural facts! In our lives too, we don't live in ignorance; we just choose to hope when there is no earthly reason for it.

Is there an area in your life where you need a reminder of hope in order to truly believe that God will bring good out of whatever you are going through? If so, write about it below:

I know hope is an area where I need to grow! The suffering and difficulty of this world can overshadow our hope if we aren't diligent in realigning ourselves with the truth of God's Word. This is why I love to study God's Word. It brings hope! Hope is key in the battle against cynicism and fear.

Make some notes below about what Abraham's faith did and didn't do as you read Romans 4:19-25:

His faith did not:	His faith did:
v. 19 *weaken*	v. 20 *strengthen*
v. 20 *waver*	v. 20 *gave glory*
	v. 21 *persuaded him*

Abraham's faith supersedes human reason and emotion. We know Abraham had some seasons of doubt, as we see when we read the biblical narrative. Don't be discouraged because your faith has wavered. God is saying that over the course of his life, Abraham held on to his faith. The general walk of his life was that of strengthening his faith. God promised Abraham a son when his wife was barren, and he believed. He grew more and more convinced over time even without evidence.

Faith often goes against our feelings. We don't always feel forgiven even when we have repented of our sin. It doesn't always seem like God protects or provides when our circumstances scream the opposite. When we believe anyway, that is faith.

As you think about your life today, how is God asking you to believe His Word against a backdrop of challenging circumstances?

Faith still believes that God's love is real when the worst happens. Faith trusts in God's strength when feeling none. This is the faith of Abraham, and it can be ours as well when we choose to believe God one moment, one hour, and one day at a time.

Let's end our time together with some great definitions of faith to encourage and strengthen our belief in God's promises.

Put a star beside the definition that most resonates with you:

"Faith is a living, unshakeable confidence in God's grace; it is so certain, that someone would die a thousand times for it. This kind of trust in and knowledge of God's grace makes a person joyful, confident, and happy with regard to God and all creatures. This is what the Holy Spirit does by faith."[11]

✷ **"Faith does not operate in the realm of the possible. There is no glory for God in that which is humanly possible. Faith begins where man's power ends."**[12]

✗ **"Faith is trust in the divine faithfulness."**[13]

"Faith means that we trust that there is someone trustworthy to keep us and preserve us in the face of danger. If we throw ourselves on God, he will always catch us."[14]

As we close, write our three key words from today's lesson below:

P _homise_

H _ope_

F _aith_

As we exercise faith in the promises of God, it brings hopeful anticipation for the future. I'm not sure where you put your X on the line indicating your general level of hope at the beginning of today's lesson, but I want to go back and move mine closer to the hopeful side! I pray you have more joyful anticipation—more hope—in whatever circumstances you find yourself today.

Talk with God

Lord, thank You for being a God who raises the dead and can bring something out of nothing. Help me to remember who You are as I process my life. Strengthen my faith and show me Your hope today. You are the promise fulfilled. Thank You for coming, dying, and rising from the grave for me. Amen.

Memory Verse Exercise

Read the Memory Verse on page 46 several times, and then fill in the blanks below as you recite it:

But __God__ demonstrates his __own love__ for us in this: __While we__ were still __sinners__, Christ died for __us__.

(Romans 5:8)

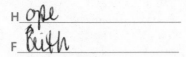

Big Idea

Even when our circumstances are puzzling, we can still place our hope in God knowing He fulfills every promise He makes.

DAY 3: HOPE THAT DOES NOT DISAPPOINT

When I received the news that I'd been invited for an interview on the 700 Club, I felt a nervous excitement. While I had done some radio interviews, I had never done anything on television. I would be speaking at an event in Phoenix and flying directly to Virginia for the taping. The day before I left, I woke up with a headache. On the plane I blew my nose hundreds of times. By God's grace, I made it through my teaching in Phoenix with a fever. I got up at 3:00 a.m. the next morning to catch my flight. When I arrived at the studio, the sweet gal took one look at me and put on a mask and gloves before doing my makeup. I think my nose resembled Rudolph's, but she did a miracle and made me look

Scripture Focus

Romans 5:1-5

presentable. I laughed with the Lord as He gave me the strength moment by moment to share what was on my heart. While I enjoyed the time, it didn't turn out as I'd expected. I was disappointed that I was so sick on what was an important day for me.

Can you think of a time when you were looking forward to something but ended up disappointed in the way it turned out? Write about it below:

Many times when it has rained - Sanibel

Today we are going to read in Romans 5 about the hope that does not disappoint. The tone of Paul's letter to the Roman Christians has been largely theological up to this point. He wanted the church to know that they were not justified by the law but by faith in Christ. Paul also spent time helping both Jews and Gentiles see their connection with one another as spiritual children of Abraham. Now we'll find Paul hitting the pause button on teaching theology. Is anyone else a little bit excited to take a deep breath and review the benefits of the spiritual words we've been discussing so far? I know I'm excited about today's verses.

Since we are covering a little less ground, I'd like us to begin by paraphrasing Romans 5:1-2 in your own words below:

Because we have faith in God we can have peace and hope. It is all through grace.

Two of the gals in the pilot study group mentioned that these verses remind them of the hymn "It Is Well with My Soul," which was written by Horatio Spafford. Spafford experienced many disappointments in his life. His son died at the age of four, and the Great Chicago Fire wiped out much of his wealth. He sent his wife and three daughters ahead to Europe while he finished some last-minute business. Their ship sank, and only his wife survived. When he sailed to join her, he penned the words to this hymn at the place where his daughters died. Though his life was filled with disappointments, he found hope in the place that never disappoints. These first verses in Romans 5 remind us of some of the blessings we can hold on to in the midst of our disappointments.

The first blessing is peace. The Greek word for peace is *eirene*, and one of the definitions is "the tranquil state of a soul assured of its salvation through Christ, and so fearing nothing from God and content with its earthly lot, of whatsoever

sort that is."[15] Does that sound good to anyone right now? We have this peace with God because of what Christ has done for us.

Think about the peace that you have with a holy, sinless God through the blood of Christ. Meditate on that truth for about a minute or so. Write any responses or reflections below:

Living in a world so full of brokenness and disfunction, having faith is what sustains me.

A second blessing we find in Romans 5:1-2 is access to God. Depending on your translation, it may say "undeserved privilege" or "introduction," but the meaning is the same. The word picture for access can be understood as an "entrance to the king through the favor of another."[16] We can enter into relationship with God through Christ.

Our family has connections through close friends with the lead singer of a very popular band. My daughter and husband were gifted tickets with VIP status to one of their concerts. They felt special and privileged even with the limited access they had to the actual performers. You and I have even greater access to the God of the universe. We can come to Him with all our questions, frustrations, and praises.

Read Hebrews 4:16 in the margin. According to this verse, what can we do because of Christ?

Come boldly to his throne

What are some tangible ways you take advantage of this access to God through Christ?

Prayer, worship

> So let us come boldly to the throne of our gracious God. There we will receive his mercy, and we will find grace to help us when we need it most.
>
> (Hebrews 4:16)

We can boldly approach God's throne of grace knowing that we will find mercy there. We can talk to God and listen to Him through His Word and His Spirit. We have unlimited access any time of the day or night!

A third blessing in these two verses is the ability to confidently and joyfully look forward to sharing God's glory. I must admit, this is hard for me to wrap my mind around. God's glory is hard to define. Do you ever wonder how we will share in it? This glory is something we will experience fully in heaven.

I want to think about glory with greater anticipation. Paul wrote in his letter to the church at Colossae that believers should think about heaven.

Read Colossians 3:1-2 in the margin. What images come to your mind as you think about heaven?

I see something very bright and full of light

Our culture sometimes references heaven with pictures of people playing harps on fluffy clouds. Others speak of it as a perpetual church service. Honestly, none of those things sound inviting to me. The Bible describes heaven as a place with streets (Revelation 21:21), houses (John 14:2), and feasts (Revelation 19:9). It is a place with no tears or trials (Revelation 21:4).

While it is difficult to envision, Paul encourages us to think about the next life to bring us hope. In his book *Heaven*, Randy Alcorn says, "Nothing is more often misdiagnosed than our homesickness for Heaven. We think that what we want is sex, drugs, alcohol, a new job, a raise, a doctorate, a spouse, a large-screen television, a new car, a cabin in the woods, a condo in Hawaii. What we really want is the person we were made for, Jesus, and the place we were made for, Heaven. Nothing less can satisfy us."[17]

What is making you homesick for heaven lately?

fear of the unknown

Realizing that our hope is found in Christ alone aligns us to eternal truths.

We aren't there yet, but realizing that our hope is found in Christ alone aligns us to eternal truths.

God has given us peace, access to Him through Christ, and the promise of future glory. Take a moment to write a brief prayer below thanking God for these three blessings that you have in Christ:

Thank you father that I can come to you at any time & that I can have peace that you will always care for me

We've seen Paul making arguments and anticipating the reaction of his audience. He seems to be doing it here in Romans 5 as well. He might have known that some people might be thinking he sounds a little "pie in the sky" when life is really hard and full of trials. After all, the Jews had been kicked out of Rome and had only returned recently under the new emperor, so they were well acquainted with suffering. Paul heads off any arguments in the next verses by teaching that these blessings are spiritual and not a promise of circumstantial comfort or ease.

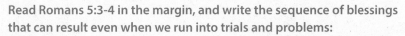

Read Romans 5:3-4 in the margin, and write the sequence of blessings that can result even when we run into trials and problems:

Problems and trials help us develop _endurance_.

Endurance develops _strength of character_

Character strengthens our _confident hope of salvation_

We've come right back to our theme for the week: *hope*.

How have endurance, character, and confident hope developed in seasons of difficulty in your life? If a circumstance from the past comes to mind, write a sentence or two about what happened and how it produced some of these qualities in your life:

Death of dad @ early age

Paul reminded the believers in Rome that suffering was a normal part of life, even for a Christian. Although God is not the author of our pain, He can use it to accomplish His purposes in our lives. Don't hear me say that we should rejoice *because* we are suffering. God keeps track of our sorrows, even storing our tears in a bottle (Psalm 56:8). God cried when His people experienced the consequences of their pride (Jeremiah 13:17), and Jesus wept when his friend Lazarus died (John 11:35). Romans 5 isn't proof that we should desire suffering; it just gives us hope that even in the midst of pain, God can produce good things. One commentator likens hope to a muscle that atrophies when it goes unused; challenges to hope can provide the resistance we need to strengthen our hope muscles.[18]

What challenges are you facing right now that have the potential to strengthen your hope muscle?

Always a tough job

Can you see God producing endurance and strength of character in your life through these trials? If so, how? If not, what invitation might God be making to you?

Each time I realize more that I can handle things

Extra Insight

If you are struggling to embrace hope, I recommend reading Philip Yancey's book *Disappointment with God*.

It takes faith to believe that God can develop our endurance and character and lead us to confident hope. It's much easier to wallow and whine while eating ice cream and watching Netflix. Okay, maybe that is just how I try to escape the pains in my life. Maybe you turn to other places when you don't want to work your hope muscle. Those times when I have set my face toward God and asked Him to grow me through trials, trusting Him to do the inner work of character development, I have found a hope that has never disappointed.

Summarize Romans 5:5 in your own words below:

> Because God has given us the Holy Spirit to guide use, we can always be hopeful

Many things in life have left me disappointed when I have expected them to fill the ache inside. I crave chocolate on a daily basis. After I indulge, I sometimes feel sick from too much or regret the impact it will have on the scale the next day. As a college student, I thought that if I could just get married and have kids, life would be amazing. Don't get me wrong, marriage and parenting is great, and I love my family; but human relationships will never ultimately fulfill the God-shaped hole in our souls. Your hopes may look much different, but they all will eventually disappoint in some way because they were never meant to leave you with lasting peace.

There are even times when we feel disappointed with God. We don't always feel the hope we've been talking about this week. Don't feel shame for having emotions but take the time to work through them. Ask questions, talk with a counselor, and explore the reasons that hope may not be resonating in your spiritual walk right now.

We can find hope that doesn't disappoint in only one place: a relationship with God. Even if we had the perfect house, the perfect body, and amazing relationships, we still would experience disappointments. Houses need maintenance, bodies get older, and every person sins and lets us down at some point. But the good news is that God says His hope will never lead us to disappointment because He loves us and has given us the Holy Spirit to fill our hearts with His love. We need only receive it!

Talk with God

Lord, I am grateful for Your peace and the access You have given me to come directly to You. Help me to understand what it means that I will one day share in Your glory. Lord, give me Your perspective as I share in Your sufferings. I long to develop endurance, strength of character, and confident hope in You. Thank You that Your hope does not disappoint. Amen.

Memory Verse Exercise

Read the Memory Verse on page 46 several times, and then fill in the blanks below as you recite it:

But ___God___ ___demonstrates___ his ___own___ ___love___ for us ___in___ ___this___ : ___While___ ___we___ were still ___sinners___ , Christ ___died___ for ___us___ .

(Romans 5:8)

DAY 4: HOPE IN CHRIST'S LIFE

Growing up in a small East Texas town, I attended kindergarten through tenth grade in the same school district. When my dad announced we were moving to a suburb of Dallas, it rocked my world. While I threw a fit about all the changes at the time, I can look back now and see how God grew me in huge ways during that season. Our family connected with a dynamic church that took discipleship seriously.

The gal who became my closest friend was a cheerleader who wanted me on the squad. Since I didn't have any cheer experience, she talked me into trying out for the mascot; and since I was the only one trying out, I got the job. At football and basketball games I wore a hawk costume and did skits for the children in the crowds. Inside the costume my eyes were level with the hawk's beak. At this time in my life God was capturing my heart in a personal way, and Romans 5:8 resonated strongly with me. So I wrote the verse on a scrap of paper and taped it inside that beak where I could see it during the games.

Romans 5:8 is our memory verse this week. Write as much of it as you can below. (Feel free to use your Bible if you need help.)

But God demonstrates his own love for us in this way; While we were still sinners, Christ died for us.

This verse encapsulates the gospel in a way that gets at the heart of my insecurities. I can talk a good grace game, but something inside of me wants to earn the love and approval of others, including God. I want to be a godly wife,

Big Idea

Though many things in life disappoint us, God's hope never will if we believe and receive it.

Scripture Focus

Romans 5:6-11

Extra Insight

Romans 5:6 reminds us that Christ came at just the right time. This gives us hope that there is a divine calendar and that God never gets His days mixed up.

loving mother, and sacrificial friend. At times my motives to live this way are the overflow of God's love in me, but other times these goals come out of a place of hoping to be accepted. I want God and others to say, "Good job."

When I read Romans 5:8, what makes me tear up every time is the phrase "While we were yet sinners." The verse on that scrap of paper in the beak of my hawk costume was written in the New International Version, so these words are forever burned in my memory even thirty years later: "But God demonstrates his own love for us in this: While we were still sinners, Christ died for us."

Here is what God didn't say:

- Because you read your Bible and pray every day
- Because you do good works
- Because other people say you are nice
- Because you got an A on your test or an accolade at work

No, God demonstrated His love by sending His Son to die for us while we were still sinners. Whenever I get off track into "work hard so God will love you" mode, the Holy Spirit whispers these words in my ear, "While Melissa was still a sinner, Christ died for her."

Write your name in the blanks below to move this truth a little closer to home:

But God demonstrates his own love for ~Georga~ in this: While ~Georga~ was still a sinner, Christ died for ~Georga O~.

How does this truth encourage you?

There is nothing greater than what he did for me

Now let's look at this verse again in context. Read Romans 5:6-11, and answer the following questions:

When did Christ come to die for us? (v. 6)

The right time - We were powerless

What makes us right in God's sight? (v. 9)

That we we justfied by his blood

What was restored by the death of God's Son? (v. 10)

Our relationship w/ them

What will we be saved through? (v. 10)

his life

Because of Jesus Christ, how can our relationship with God be described? (v. 11)

Reconciled

Your translation may use the word *reconciliation* in verse 11 to describe this new relationship. The King James version uses the word *atonement*. The New Living translation uses the word *friends*. The Greek word for *reconciled* in verse 10 is *katallasso*, which means "to change, exchange, as coins for others of equivalent value; to reconcile (those who are at variance); return to favour with, be reconciled to one; to receive one into favour."[19] I like the picture of exchanging enemy status or separation from God because of sin to friendship with God through Christ. Knowing that we can be a friend of God, or reconciled to God through Christ, brings us great hope. Yet friendship with God is different than friendship with a "buddy." While our friends are our peers and equals, "friendship with God" does not convey that aspect of human friendship.

Here are some friendship parallels that we *can* connect to our relationship with God.

Circle the aspect of friendship that you most relate to in your relationship with God right now:

- **Friends spend time together**
- **Friends tell each other their secrets**
-  **Friends are honest and trustworthy**
- **Friends like each other**

We use the term *friend* pretty loosely in our culture. We can have thousands of "friends" on social media and not even be able to recall their names or even recognize them if we saw them in a crowd. The picture here is one of exchange. We were once at odds, but the blood of Christ accomplished the payment for our sin. Reconciliation is a major theme of the entire letter to the Romans. We find that we can come close to a holy God because of Christ.

Romans 5:10 says that we were restored by the death of Christ and saved by the life of Christ. What do you think this means?

He had to rise again for us to be saved

Major Ian Thomas wrote a book called *The Saving Life of Christ* that helped me understand this better. Like me, Major Thomas wanted to work hard for God after he encountered the love and grace of Christ. For seven years he did just that, describing himself as a windmill of activity that led him to complete spiritual and physical exhaustion. He became bitter and discouraged. Through tears he sensed the Lord saying this to him: "You see, for seven years, with utmost sincerity, you have been trying to live *for* Me, on My behalf, the life that I have been waiting for seven years to live *through* you."[20] This was revelatory for Major Thomas and changed the course of his life. He stopped trying to live in His own strength and, instead, yielded and depended on God for the energy, direction, and power to live. He taught that while Christ's death saves us from the penalty of sin, it is His life that enables us to live the Christian life.

Major Thomas did not find this dependence on Christ to be one of inactivity or complacency. In fact, he did amazing things over the course of his life. Before he died, I was able to hear him speak about this topic at my church outside Dallas during my high school mascot years.

Read the Scriptures below, and underline any phrases that support the idea that God is the source of our power for living the Christian life:

[23]*Now may the God of peace make you holy in every way, and may your whole spirit and soul and body be kept blameless until our Lord Jesus Christ comes again.* [24]*God will make this happen, for he who calls you is faithful.*

(1 Thessalonians 5:23-24)

For God is working in you, giving you the desire and the power to do what pleases him.

(Philippians 2:13)

So God Himself empowers us to live the Christian life in our daily walk. But practically speaking, how do we stop trying to live *for* God and, instead, let Christ live His life *through* us? It is an important nuance that gets to the heart of our thoughts and motives.

Some examples of allowing Christ to live through us might be

- having a general focus on "being" instead of "doing"
- taking extended time to pray and listen to God (especially about where to serve)
- depending less on our human logic and more on our prayer lives when making decisions
- valuing rest and relationship as much as activity

What are some other examples of allowing Christ to live through us?

Where or how do you need God to infuse you with His power for living today?

All of the 4 bullets above are a struggle for me

The saving life of Christ is more about internal posture changes that impact our motives and thoughts rather than action steps. I like action steps, so I need this lesson about abiding in Christ rather than working on His behalf!

One of the practical ways I've tried to stop living for God and allow Christ to live through me pertains to the questions I ask myself in my internal dialogue. I have the opportunity to teach the Bible in cities all over the country, and my tendency afterward is to say in my heart, "How did I do?" Then one day I received good counsel to change that question to "Who am I becoming?" Just changing that question in my internal conversation with myself has helped me abide more fully in Christ and fight the tendency to measure my work for Him.

Is there an area in your life and ministry where your internal questions need to change? Think and pray on that for a moment, and write any ideas that come to mind:

My relationships & colleagues What kind of colleague am I and can I be for 4 more years

The gals who piloted this study had some great examples I want to share with you:

When we see Christ as the One empowering us through His Holy Spirit, it takes the pressure off.

From:

Why did they do that?

What's their problem?

How will this impact my day?

To:

How can I be a blessing to them?

Where are they coming from?

How will this matter in eternity?

When we see Christ as the One empowering us through His Holy Spirit, it takes the pressure off. We don't have to figure it all out and do it all right. Instead, we ask God to do it in us and through us. Jesus didn't save us by His death and resurrection and then leave us on our own. He continues to empower us as we find hope through His life. We can lean into Him for strength and wisdom for each day.

Talk with God

Lord, You are truly the God of hope. Through the death and life of Christ You have provided everything I need for this life and the next. Help me to stop spinning my wheels with activity so that I feel productive. Show me what it means to rest in You and allow You to live Your life through mine. Amen.

Big Idea

Christ died for us and wants us not to work for Him but to allow Him to work through us.

Memory Verse Exercise

Read the Memory Verse on page 46 several times, and then fill in the blanks below as you recite it:

But God demonstrates his own love for us in this : While we were still sinners, Christ died for us

(*Romans 5:8*)

DAY 5: HOPE IN THE SECOND ADAM

Scripture Focus

Romans 5:12-21

During my childhood my mother had a garden where we grew cucumbers, tomatoes, and peppers. I would help weed, water, and gather the bounty. When my children were little, I decided we needed a garden so that my children could learn about where their food came from as well as discover the many connections between gardening and spiritual realities. My husband borrowed a rototiller

and prepared a large square in the backyard. We divided the square into four smaller squares so that each child had an area to grow, weed, water, and gather. I saw visions of the lessons they would learn and the pride they would have in their accomplishments. Somehow it didn't go the way I had envisioned.

We proclaimed "weeding Wednesday" as the day when everyone's patch had to be finished before we could leave for the pool. One particularly hot day as the children were working, one of them asked me why weeds grow so much. I told them that part of the curse of sin in Genesis had to do with making the ground difficult to work, pointing out that the Scripture even mentions thorns and thistles growing as a consequence (Genesis 3:17-19). Later I heard one of them hacking away at the ground saying, "Why did Adam do it? Why did he bring this curse?" I chuckled at their dramatic overture and grew to dislike weeding Wednesday as much as the children. After several years of more complaining than satisfaction in our gardening attempts, we reseeded that section of the yard and grew grass.

In our reading today, we will go all the way back to the first garden. Paul's message brings hope for the predicament sin brought on the planet through Adam. And weeds are just the tip of the iceberg when it comes to consequences of the curse.

Read Romans 5:12-14 below, and fill in the blanks that follow with words or simple pictures. I've done the first one for you.

¹²*When Adam sinned, sin entered the world. Adam's sin brought death, so death spread to everyone, for everyone sinned.* ¹³*Yes, people sinned even before the law was given. But it was not counted as sin because there was not yet any law to break.* ¹⁴*Still, everyone died—from the time of Adam to the time of Moses—even those who did not disobey an explicit commandment of God, as Adam did. Now Adam is a symbol, a representation of Christ, who was yet to come.*

sinned.

Sin entered the _____.

Sin brought _____.

People sinned even before _____ was given.

Adam is a symbol, a representation of _____.

Extra Insight

Adam Christology is the theological term used to describe the concept in Romans 5:12-14.

Paul went back to the beginning to help us understand the good news about hope against the backdrop of the bad news about sin. By beginning with Adam, he forced his readers to look at the big picture. After yesterday's study on hope, this talk of Adam and sin might seem a little anticlimactic, but hang in there with me. Our understanding of Adam and Christ helps shape our worldview.

If we don't understand our relation to Adam, we are missing the complete picture of the greatness of our salvation. We can't fully appreciate Christ's work on the cross until we grasp the depravity of sin. The doctrine of original sin is one that some people don't like, but G. K. Chesterton famously said, "Original sin is the only Christian doctrine that is empirically verifiable. All people sin."[21]

I never had to teach my children to behave selfishly or fight with one another. They seemed to instinctively know how. Sin came through the first man. As we talk about the depravity of humanity, we must balance it with the image of God that we all bear. While sin affected humankind greatly, we remember that we were created in God's image. We need balance in recognizing the impact of both the image of God and the effects of sin. Paul presents Adam as a representation of Christ; however, they are markedly different.

Read Romans 5:15-19 and label each statement "A" for Adam or "C" for Christ:

_A_ The sin of this man brought death to many.

_C_ God's wonderful grace and forgiveness came through this man.

_A_ This man's sin led to condemnation.

_C_ Even though people are guilty of many sins, this man made a way for us to become right with God.

_A_ This man's sin caused death to rule over many.

_C_ Those who receive the gift of righteousness through this man will triumph over sin and death.

_A_ Because this person disobeyed God, many became sinners.

_C_ Because this person obeyed God, many will become righteous.

Did you notice the pattern of Adam followed by Christ throughout? Did you also notice the words "even greater" used more than once in this passage? Adam brought condemnation for everyone, but Christ brought a right relationship with God. His grace and power is even greater than the power of sin. Now that is good news!

We understand the redemption story only when we understand what was lost. Many of the stories of our culture mimic this classic story of something lost and then redeemed. Milton's *Paradise Lost* and *Paradise Regained* are classic pieces of literature that tell the story of Romans 5:12-21. In an interview, George Lucas said that "the entire Star Wars trilogy—or at least the first trilogy—was concerned with the redemption of Anakin Skywalker. One could say that the entire story line of redemptive history is about the redemption of Adam."[22]

What other books, movies, or real life stories that contain a redemptive theme come to mind for you?

This account of Adam and Christ in Romans 5 not only gives us the big picture but also illustrates the hope that doesn't disappoint. We find hope in a new and living way.

Read 1 Corinthians 15:22 in the margin. What will be given to everyone who belongs to Christ?

new life

Just as everyone dies because we all belong to Adam, everyone who belongs to Christ will be given new life.
(1 Corinthians 15:22)

We have been promised new life in Christ. This hope certainly applies to this life for we have been given power over sin, purpose in sharing the message of God's love, and community with other believers. However, we are still living in the weeds to a certain extent. Thankfully, our hope extends far beyond this life.

Read Romans 5:20-21 and summarize these verses in a few sentences below: *The law came about to draw out the sin but as sin increased Gods grace increased more through salvation*

How does this good news of God's grace give you hope personally? *We will always sin but God's grace is always sufficient*

Through Christ, grace rules. The law has served its purpose in showing us our sin.

Now read 1 Corinthians 15:53-57 below, and underline any hopeful words or phrases that stand out to you:

⁵³For our dying bodies must be transformed into bodies that will never die; our mortal bodies must be transformed into <u>immortal bodies</u>.

⁵⁴Then, when our dying bodies have been transformed into bodies that will never die, this Scripture will be fulfilled:

"<u>Death is swallowed up</u> in victory.
⁵⁵O death, where is your victory?
O death, where is your sting?"

⁵⁶For sin is the sting that results in death, and the law gives sin its power. ⁵⁷But thank God! He gives us <u>victory over sin and death</u> through our Lord Jesus Christ.

These verses parallel Romans 5:20-21, reminding us that <u>in the darkest corner of the room a candle shines the brightest. In the blackest night of our sin, God's grace shines forth, filling us with hope for the future.</u>

Tell how this good news about Christ give you hope in regard to:

Your family: *God has & will continue to guide us w/ parents*

Your friends: *I pray regularly for + changes for Patty & Michele*

Your health: *I trust that God will provide care in old age*

Your work:

Your ministry/service:

Other: _____

The narrative the Lord longs to write in our lives is redemptive in nature. Christ wants to shine life into all of your relationships. We can find hope for our broken bodies in remembering we will get new ones in eternity! When things

The narrative the Lord longs to write in our lives is redemptive in nature.

are tough at work, we can remember that every person sins, so we shouldn't expect perfection from others. Instead we can live with a "grace rules" mindset and bring hope to others. In every area of life, we can find a reason to hope when we view it through the lens of Christ. He replaced the sin and death that came through Adam with life and peace.

We must be intentional to believe these truths by faith, yet this is easier said than done. We still live daily with the effects of sin. Sin brings death to relationships, bodies, and communities. So, in order to experience the hope of the verses we've read today, we must be intentional to dwell on them regularly and allow them to transform our perspective.

What are some practical things you can do to keep these hopeful gospel truths central in your thinking as you process the challenging effects of sin that surround you?

Write them on a note card
Post them
Devotions

Talking to godly friends, attending church and small group Bible studies, and reading God's Word regularly are some things that help me stay aligned to this hopeful message. You may have additional ways of keeping gospel truths central in your life. Whatever practices we use, this good news truly changes everything when we allow it to sink deep into our souls; so let's lean in and embrace every bit of this hope today!

Talk with God

Lord, help me to see the big picture. Help me to be aware of my worldview. Let Your truth shape it more than the culture in which I live. Thank You for sending Christ as the second Adam to redeem me. Show me how to walk in hope this week because of all You have done. Amen.

Memory Verse Exercise

Read the Memory Verse on page 46 several times, and then fill in the blanks below as you recite it:

But God demonstrated his own love for us in this : While we were still sinners, Christ died for us.

(Romans 5:8)

Big Idea

Adam brought condemnation for everyone, but Christ brought a right relationship with God.

Weekly Wrap Up

Review the Big Idea for each day, and then write any personal application that comes to mind.

Day 1: Hope in a Family
Big Idea: We find hope by being connected to a larger family of faith as children of Abraham.

Personal Application:_____

_____

Day 2: Against All Hope
Big Idea: Even when our circumstances are puzzling, we can still place our hope in God knowing He fulfills every promise He makes.

Personal Application:_____

_____

Day 3: Hope That Does Not Disappoint
Big Idea: Though many things in life disappoint us, God's hope never will if we believe and receive it.

Personal Application:_____

_____

Day 4: Hope in Christ's Life
Big Idea: Christ died for us and wants us not to work for Him but to allow Him to work through us.

Personal Application:_____

_____

Day 5: Hope in the Second Adam
Big Idea: Adam brought condemnation for everyone, but Christ brought a right relationship with God.

Personal Application:_____

_____

VIDEO VIEWER GUIDE: WEEK 2

GOOD NEWS ABOUT HOPE

Hebrews 6:18-19

Our faith becomes _____ as we recognize our need for a _____.

Romans 3:23-24

Even when we have no reason for hope, we hope because of what _____ has
_____.

Romans 4:16-18

Romans 5:1-2

_____ have the power to lead us to hope.

Romans 5:3-6

Week 3

Good News About Daily Life

Romans 6–8

Memory Verse

And I am convinced that nothing can ever separate us from God's love. Neither death nor life, neither angels nor demons, neither our fears for today nor our worries about tomorrow—not even the powers of hell can separate us from God's love.

(Romans 8:38)

DAY 1: INDEPENDENCE DAY

Scripture Focus

Romans 6:1-23

I don't know what your typical day is like, but when I'm not traveling and speaking mine can include a lot of minutia: unloading and reloading the dishwasher, running a few loads of laundry, sifting through a ton of emails, reading commentaries or writing, chatting with my sister on the phone, and of course…Jazzercise (my exercise of choice)! Your work schedule, parenting responsibilities, or retirement season might cause your typical day to look much different than mine. Many times our routines can feel repetitive and boring, and other times we hit milestones and celebrate exciting news. In the midst of it all, we want to grow in our faith and become more like Jesus. How do we invite Him into household chores, work commutes, and potty-training? This week we'll explore Paul's words to the church at Rome in chapters 6–8 and see how we can apply theological truths in our daily lives.

In chapters 1–5, Paul focused on the foundational principle that we are saved from the penalty of sin (justification). As we open Romans 6 today, we'll find him speaking about where the rubber meets the road as we navigate what it means to be saved practically from the power of sin (sanctification). It helps me to sort out these theological terms by thinking of salvation like this:

- Justification means I have *been saved* from the *penalty* of sin.
- Sanctification means I am *being saved* from the *power* of sin.
- Glorification means one day I *will be saved* from the *presence* of sin.

Those statements are chock full of good news for you and me!

My husband and I are in the early stages of building a house. Before anything else can happen, a solid foundation must be built. Without that important element, the work in the house above will be in vain. We can pick the best floors, countertops, and cabinets, but if the foundation isn't strong, then everything else will be affected.

Our sanctification (daily walk with Christ) is like the living space of our spiritual lives. In our living rooms, kitchens, and bedrooms, we make a wealth of day-to-day decisions about how to spend our thoughts, time, and resources. While sin impacts our lives, God longs to empower us to overcome it.

Read Romans 6:1-11 and fill in the following blanks according to the passage. (Refer to the New Living Translation if possible.)

1. You have ___died___ to sin. (v. 2)

Digging Deeper

This week we'll find many references to baptism in Romans 6–8. For a deeper look at the historical background of Christian baptism, check out the Digging Deeper article for Week 3, "Dive" (see AbingdonWomen.com/Romans).

While sin impacts our lives, God longs to empower us to overcome it.

2. Because we were raised with Christ, we can live _new_ lives. (v. 4)

3. We are no longer _slaves_ to sin. (v. 6)

4. We have been set free from the _power_ of sin. (v. 7)

5. You can consider yourself _dead_ to sin and _alive_ to God. (v. 11)

How do these verses ring true—or conflict—with your daily battle with sin? Write any thoughts or questions you have below:

It does not feel like were dead to it when we face our sins and shortcomings

These verses are profound statements about what God has done. God has said we are no longer dominated by sin. It no longer has the power to rule in our lives. Christ's death, burial, and resurrection brought about our independence day from the tyranny of sin. On July fourth we celebrate our country's freedom to worship, work, and live. We set off fireworks and have parades to mark our independence to rule ourselves. Yet each of us decides whether we will use our national freedoms to serve, work, and contribute to our free society, or whether we will use our freedoms in less productive ways.

In the same way, we are free from the dominion of sin, but we live in a world still under sin's curse. We must not live as though we are under the control of an old regime, but we must acknowledge the fact that we live in overlapping ages. The new age of grace has come through Christ, and we no longer live under the law. However, sin still besets us. I must admit that sanctification can be confusing for me at times, and here is why: God says I am no longer dominated by sin because of what Christ has done, but I find myself in a daily power struggle with sin. Can you relate?

My desire is to pray and study the Bible, but my flesh says to sleep longer and watch TV instead. This victory we read about doesn't come by default. One commentator said it this way, "The victory over sin that God has won for us in Christ is a victory that must be appropriated."[1] So we have a role to play in making choices when it comes to our sanctification. Yet it is God who does the work in us.

Read Romans 6:12-14 and put a checkmark beside the instructions that Paul gave the believers in these verses:

✓ 1. Do not let sin control you

_____ 2. Do not eat too much ice cream

✓ 3. Do not give in to sinful desires

✓ 4. Do not use your body as an instrument of evil

_____ 5. Do whatever you want because you are free

✓ 6. Give yourselves completely to God

✓ 7. Use your body as an instrument to do what is right for the glory of God

_____ 8. It is okay to sin a lot because it will all be forgiven anyway

✓ 9. Don't live with sin as your master but live instead under the freedom of God's grace

As you think about these instructions, what are some practices that help you live out these commands? In other words, what helps you *not* to give in to sin—whether the battle is in your mind, words, attitudes, or actions?

> Prayer
> Try to keep verses close by
> Avoid certain situations

The gals in the pilot study shared these ideas:

- Pausing to pray, and practicing regular prayer
- Minimizing or avoiding social media
- Taking time for discernment rather than making rash decisions
- Journaling
- Holding my tongue
- Reading/studying Scripture
- Spending time with other believers
- Serving others
- Worshiping
- Taking time for silence and rest

Our answers may be different, because God helps us in many different ways; but I've found that trying harder or focusing on behavior modification sets me up for even more failure. Incorporating spiritual rhythms is what helps me to

Answers: You should have checked 1, 3, 4, 6, 7, and 9.

offer myself to God—to consent to His presence and work within me—rather than to offer myself to sin. These include things such as praying, resting, studying and memorizing God's Word, and spending time with other believers. We cannot forget that we have a role to play—not one of trying to overcome sin in our own strength but one of using our freedom well.

Speaking of freedom, Paul used slavery as a metaphor to explain our victory in Christ since it was something that affected the lives of the Romans. Many in the church could have been slaves themselves.

> **Read Romans 6:15-23 and explain this metaphor below. What does it mean to be set free from slavery to sin and become a slave to righteous living?**

you are still ruled by something/someone but now it's for good

Extra Insight

We can't understate the impact of slavery on Roman culture. "Slavery was a basic reality in Greco-Roman society....According to varying estimates from one-fifth to one-third of the population was enslaved."[2] Those are staggering numbers.

Paul used this terrible practice that was common in his day to help us understand our relationship with sin. He reminds us that we are slaves of whatever we choose to obey. We can become a slave to righteous living if we offer ourselves to God, who then empowers us to make choices that lead to life, joy, and peace.

After studying Romans 6, I want to have more victory over sin in my life. I wonder if you do too. The good news about our daily walk with Christ is that we don't have to figure it out on our own. Verse 23 says, "For the wages of sin is death, but the free gift of God is eternal life through Christ Jesus our Lord." We have a Savior who loves us and died for us, and He longs to help us continually have victory over sin. He promises to do the work in us as we yield ourselves to Him.

Here's a final and important point as we wrap up today. While justification happens in a moment, our sanctification takes place over a lifetime. It includes growth spurts and seasons where we lose ground. It can feel like three steps forward and two steps back, but over time we find greater freedom and less slavery to sin as we keep walking in faith.

I used to think of sanctification like this:

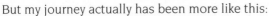

But my journey actually has been more like this:

We need to remember that the process of sanctification has highs and lows. Many times the lows propel us into the growth. Other times there are plateaus where not much seems to be progressing spiritually. So, no matter where you've found yourself lately in the battle against sin and the journey of sanctification, I want to remind you that each new day is your independence day from sin! While we live in overlapping ages, we are no longer dominated by sin's power through Christ. Now *that* is good news that changes everything!

Talk with God

Lord, I offer myself fully to You. Help me to focus on You so that I won't be tempted to fix my gaze on lesser things. I need Your help in the battle against sin in my life. I want to become what You have already made me to be through Christ. Thank You for the power over sin that You promise in Your Word. Amen.

Memory Verse Exercise

Read the Memory Verse on page 76 several times, and then fill in the blanks below as you recite it:

And *I am convinced that* **nothing** *can ever separate us from God's* **love** *. Neither death nor life, neither* **angels** *nor demons, neither our fears for today nor our worries about tomorrow—not even the powers of hell can separate us from God's love.*

(Romans 8:38)

Big Idea

God has given us power over sin and calls us to walk daily in that truth by faith.

DAY 2: THE FAILURE OF LEGALISM

My husband, Sean, periodically goes on an eating plan our friends and family refer to as the "Sean Spoelstra" diet. It is basically no soda, candy, dessert, or eating after 8:00 p.m. He did this for the entire year when he turned thirty and

Scripture Focus

Romans 7:1-13

again when he turned forty. Now, my husband is such a rule-follower that if he had almost finished eating a piece of toast and the clock turned 8:01 p.m., he would put it down and not finish it.

I got a lot of mileage out of teasing him for his food legalism. (I might have used the word "Pharisee" once or twice.) He would often point out to me that it was a personal legalism—he wasn't imposing his food rules on anyone else. I had to admit the truth in that statement.

A restrictive eating plan can be beneficial for a season, just as orthodontics that straighten teeth. However, unless a limited diet is necessary for an ongoing medical condition, it usually does not work well as a way of life. That's what we will find Paul communicating with the church in Rome in our study today. We've seen that in chapter 6 of Paul's letter he warns against license. He wants the believers to understand that grace doesn't mean living lawless lives. Now in chapter 7, he points out the other extreme: legalism. We can all swing back and forth between these postures when it comes to our faith.

Label one side of the pendulum "License" and the other side "Legalism" according to the phrases in the circles:

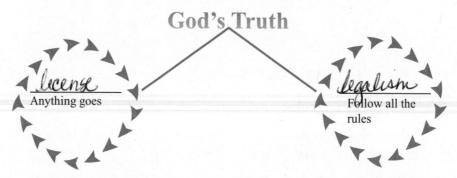

Paul wanted the church to beware of these two extremes. Avoiding these extremes is a battle we still fight today, both as individuals and as communities of believers.

Have you ever encountered a church culture that swung toward either license or legalism? If so, write about it below, including the impact it had on your faith:

Either this was a quick exercise for you, or you might be thinking you could write a book about your experience with legalism or license.

When I was in high school, a group of new families came to our church. They were kind and seemed really serious about their faith. However, they would not let their children participate in our high school Sunday school classes, and so they started their own homeschool Sunday school class. Over time and through many conversations, I began to feel labeled as a "public school girl who wore pants." (The girls in their group wore only skirts.) They were part of a homeschool cooperative with a strong leader that they quoted as much or more than the Bible. They followed a lot of rules but lacked grace in many areas. This was my first personal encounter with legalism. During this season I was growing in faith and reading through the New Testament on my own for the first time. My experience with these families left me feeling judged and confused. What I saw in their lives didn't match up with the Jesus I was encountering in the Gospels.

Warren Wiersbe defines legalism in his Romans commentary as "the belief that I can become holy and please God by obeying laws. It is measuring spirituality by a list of dos and don'ts."[3] Extreme legalism can sometimes be easier to identify, but we must guard against the subtle ways that it can creep into our spiritual rhythms. God knows our human tendency to want to check boxes.

Prayed ✔
Read the Bible ✔
Went to church ✔
Did a good deed ✔

When we mark these off in our minds, we can start feeling pretty good about ourselves. As we get good at being good, we also get good at being judgmental. While spiritual rhythms and practices are wonderful, we must be careful not to view them as a checklist. Emotional and spiritual damage can occur when we are in a system that sets a high standard of rule-following as our way to be holy and accepted in God's sight. This can lead to posing on the outside, knowing that we are failing on the inside, or to giving up altogether and walking away from the Lord and His people. Through the years I've kept up with some high school friends from that group of families that would only interact with a public school girl on a limited basis, and I've seen some of them struggle with authenticity and others completely walk away from faith.

So how do we elevate God's good instructions for us without falling into a legalistic system?

Read Romans 7:1-6 and answer the following questions:

What metaphor does Paul use to explain a believer's relationship with the law? (vv. 2-3)

A married woman when widowed is released from the law

What point does Paul say he is trying to make with this illustration? (v. 4)

We also died to the law

What is the old way to serve God? (v. 6)

Legalistically

What is the new way? (v. 6)

By the spirit

Our union with Christ produces spiritual fruit—not through rule-keeping but through the work of God in our lives.

The marriage metaphor teaches us about the believer's relationship with the law. This isn't meant to be a prescriptive teaching on marriage. Once again Paul takes a familiar institution and uses it to illustrate spiritual truth. He likens the death of a husband freeing a woman from the commitment to marriage to the coming of Christ freeing us from the power of sinful desires aroused by the law. However, all metaphors have a falling off point; and in this comparison the husband dies while the law itself is still around. We don't look to the Law for salvation, but we still have moral obligations and commands to obey as followers of God under the New Covenant. In fact, Romans 7:4 mentions our responsibility to produce fruit or a harvest of good deeds from being united to Christ. Just as marriage can bring forth children as a result, so our union with Christ produces spiritual fruit—not through rule-keeping but through the work of God in our lives.

Read the following verses and underline the force behind the fruit that is created:

"Yes, I [Christ] am the vine; you are the branches. Those who remain in me, and I in them, will produce much fruit. For apart from me you can do nothing."

(John 15:5)

²²But the <u>Holy Spirit</u> produces this kind of fruit in our lives: love, joy, peace, patience, kindness, goodness, faithfulness, ²³gentleness, and self-control. There is no law against these things!

(Galatians 5:22-23)

So even if the marriage metaphor doesn't totally flow into perfect boxes, it is important to look for the overarching parallel rather than critique the nitty gritty details. This sounds similar to our fight against legalism!

I love the way Jesus addresses the dangers of rule-following in Matthew 23:23-24:

²³"What sorrow awaits you teachers of religious law and you Pharisees. Hypocrites! For you are careful to tithe even the tiniest income from your herb gardens, but you ignore the more important aspects of the law—justice, mercy, and faith. You should tithe, yes, but do not neglect the more important things. ²⁴Blind guides! You strain your water so you won't accidentally swallow a gnat, but you swallow a camel!"

What metaphor does Jesus use in these verses when it comes to the dangers of legalism?

Swallowing a Camel

How would you summarize the point He is trying to make with the Pharisees?

justice, mercy, and faith are more important that these legalistic things

How can you apply this in your own daily walk when it comes to balancing obedience to God's Word with living in freedom from rules?

I can do my devotions & pray but if I am not kind & merciful, it means nothing

My summary of Jesus's point would be, "<u>Don't focus on minutia and miss the big picture</u>." When I read His harsh reaction to the Pharisees, I almost wonder why God even gave us the law—though I actually know why (more on that in just a bit). We need to remember that the recipients of this letter would have had great respect for the law. Certainly Jewish believers revered the law, but Gentile believers also respected it as given by the God they now worshiped.

Read Romans 7:7-13 and write below the commandment Paul uses as an example of the law in verse 7:

Do not covet

I think it's interesting that instead of using murder, stealing, or adultery, Paul picks the last of the Ten Commandments: coveting. Jealousy stands apart in the list of rules as an inward attitude, not an outward action. Paul says the command itself stirs up desire.

Can you relate to wanting to break the rules once they are stated? Often we can respond like a child. A child may have never thought to pick the flowers, but once you say, "Don't pick the flowers," that child has a sudden, strong urge to yank those pretty things right out of the ground. The rule itself seems to create our desire to break it. Paul says the law isn't the cause of that desire. It just reveals it.

I thought of an MRI machine as I read these verses. When one of our twins was five years old, I brought her to the emergency room because she was struggling to breathe and had a fever. After hours of wondering and waiting to see what was wrong, an MRI revealed she had pneumonia in both lungs with fluid built up on one side. That fluid was infected with the strep virus, which caused her little body to go into septic shock.

The MRI machine didn't create these serious health issues for our little girl. It merely revealed them. We didn't get angry at the MRI. In a similar way, the law is not inherently the problem but the identifier of the problem of sin. It cannot heal our sin struggle, just as an MRI machine could not treat my daughter's illness. So, we must see the law the way God does and not elevate or devalue it for the purpose it serves.

We must beware of throwing out the law completely. Jesus didn't. He said, "I tell you the truth, until heaven and earth disappear, not even the smallest detail of God's law will disappear until its purpose is achieved" (Matthew 5:18). Dying to the law doesn't mean we never obey it. As one source points out, "It simply means that the *motivation* and *dynamic* of our lives does not come from the law: It comes from God's grace through our union with Christ."[5]

How would you explain the purpose of the law based on our lesson today? *A guide for how we should live and want to*

Turn back to the pendulum on page 82. In light of our study today, where do you see yourself? Are you more in danger of swinging toward legalism or license in your daily life, and why? *middle- maybe my political leanings*

What helps you obey God's Word and practice spiritual rhythms without becoming legalistic?

prayer

That last question might have been challenging. What does help? Have you found deeper connection with God through meditating on Scripture, praying, practicing silence, or worshiping through song? I know I have. I believe as we continually renew our minds with truth and fellowship with other Christians we can fall into step with the Spirit of God and seek balance when it comes to embracing both truth and grace simultaneously.

Talk with God

Lord Jesus, I am prone to extremes. Help me not to reduce my relationship with You to checking boxes. When I get good at being good, reveal my desperate need for You so that I won't judge others self-righteously. Continually teach me according to Your truth, and bring Your Holy Spirit fruit in my life as I depend on You. Amen.

Memory Verse Exercise

Read the Memory Verse on page 76 several times, and then fill in the blanks below as you recite it:

And I am convinced that ___convinced___ can ever ___separate___ us from God's ___love___. Neither death nor life, neither ___angels___ nor demons, neither our ___fears___ for today nor our ___worries___ about tomorrow—not even the ___powers___ of hell can ___separate___ us from God's love.
(Romans 8:38)

Big Idea

We need a clear understanding of the purpose of God's law so that we don't veer to the side of legalism or license as we follow Jesus daily.

DAY 3: STRUGGLING BUT NOT CONDEMNED

My husband and I dropped off our twin daughters in two different cities a few months ago so they could begin their freshman year of college. Their older brother is in his fourth year at college a few hours away. We have one teenager left at home, and boy do things feel weird around the Spoelstra house. We went from loud, crazy, and bustling with activity to a strange quiet and relative calm.

Scripture Focus

Romans 7:14–8:4

Some days I love the peace and others I feel the ache of separation from my children—and even miss the chaos.

You might say that our college kids are living in "overlapping ages." On the one hand, they are autonomous and not being monitored daily. Yet at the same time, they still very much need us. I am writing these words from the waiting room as one of my college daughters undergoes a minor surgery. I can't imagine her navigating the insurance questions—not to mention her post-op care—without her momma around. College students often have one foot in adulthood and the other in childhood. They are independent but also dependent.

As believers, we understand overlapping ages. We have one foot in heaven, knowing we are free from the penalty of sin through Christ. Our other foot is on earth battling sin on a daily basis. We are free but also still under the effects of the curse. Paul has been helping the Roman believers understand that Christ has freed them from sin through His death and resurrection, yet at the same time they are still battling temptation daily. I've heard it said that believers live in the state of "already, not yet." We have already been saved from the *penalty* of sin through Christ, which is justification. We are not yet fully saved from the *power* of sin as we navigate daily life, which is sanctification.

The verses we will look at today are some that have always resonated in my life because I can relate to what Paul shares.

Read Romans 7:14-25 and correct the following false statements by writing the correct words above the words that are marked through to make the sentences true. I've done the first one for you.

the law   me
The trouble is not with ~~me~~ but with ~~the law~~. (v. 14)

I do what is not right
I want to do what is right and ~~that is what I do~~. (v. 15)

good
My awareness that I'm doing wrong proves that the law is ~~bad~~. (v. 16)

wrong   *sin*
I am not the one doing ~~right~~, it is the ~~goodness~~ living in me. (v. 17)

good
Nothing ~~bad~~ lives in me, that is, in my sinful nature. (v. 18)

I want to do what is ~~bad~~ *good*, but I don't. I don't want to do what is ~~good~~ *bad*, but I do it anyway. (v. 19)

My mind and the power of sin are at ~~peace~~ *war* within me. (v. 23)

Oh what a ~~happy~~ *wretched* person I am because of this battle inside. (v. 24)

How does verse 25 describe the answer or victory for the battle inside of us? *Thanks to God I am a slave to Gods law*

Commentators debate whether Paul was speaking of a former battle when he lived under the strict practice of rule-following as a Pharisee (Acts 23:6) or of his experience as a mature Christ-follower. No matter what season of his own life Paul was referring to, we can't deny that the struggle against sin continues for even the most seasoned Christian, highlighting our need to continually surrender to Christ and live from our identity in Him.

As you read Paul's description of the war within, can you relate with his struggle? In what ways? *Every time I do/say something thoughtless or stupid I wonder why and why I can't learn*

Sometimes it can feel like there is a tug of war inside us. We want to do right, but we need God's help to do it. As we struggle, God's love doesn't change. As this week's memory verse assures us, nothing can separate us from His love! These verses in Romans 7 give me hope that I am not alone in wanting to do what is right yet struggling to live it out consistently. I want to show kindness to my family members, but many times kindness doesn't describe my interactions. I desire to develop a godly thought-life but battle against judging others. These are just a few examples of ways that this principle plays out in my daily experience. By acknowledging the power of sin and the "flesh" or "sinful nature" (which is our natural way of living apart from God), we can then lean into God's strength, rather than our own strength, to overcome it and live in the Spirit (more on that in just a bit).

Paul's words about our struggle with sin don't give us an excuse. We can't say, "See, I can't help it," or "It's not the real me doing that bad stuff. It is my flesh or sinful nature." Explanations and excuses are two very different things. Paul still takes personal responsibility for his actions but also explains his struggle with the flesh. This explanation of our flesh or sinful nature helps us identify and understand our struggle as human beings living in a world of sin.

How have you struggled with sin in your life lately?

I think I am better than other especially at work. I say unkind things about others

Do you know that feeling when you lay your head on the pillow and review the day's bad food choices, poor time management, or harsh words you wish you could take back? I'm thankful that Paul didn't leave his readers hanging with the news that we will struggle with sin and the flesh until the day when we leave this earth and are saved from the very presence of sin. We find a stark contrast in the next verse. He begins chapter 8 with a verse chock full of hope!

Write Romans 8:1 below: *Therefore there is now no condemnation for those who are in Christ Jesus*

Extra Insight

"One of the marks of Luther's theology is the recognition that the believer is, as the famous Latin phrase has it, *simul justus et peccator*, 'at the same time just and a sinner.'"[6] This is not a statement about our identity but an acknowledgment of the practical realities of daily life. We all are still in the process of being sanctified.

After strong words about sin, Paul transitions to a strong statement against condemnation! At times we may feel convicted of sin, which leads us toward God in repentance, but we never have to embrace condemnation. Though we still struggle with sin, we are no longer condemned. Because of Christ, we are free from condemnation.

Read Romans 8:2-4 and summarize these truths in a sentence or two:

By sending his own son in the likeness of a sinful man, Christ overcame the sinful nature

We are now free to follow the Holy Spirit of God rather than our flesh or sinful nature. Sin can be discouraging, and we all fall into its trap from time to time. Fighting temptation in our own strength will leave us defeated. Yet by the power of the Spirit, we have the ability to live new lives. We can overcome sin and follow God's way through His Spirit living in us.

As we allow these theological truths to sink deep, we find ourselves thinking more correctly about God, sin, others, and ourselves. Today's verses help us to

- understand our struggle with sin. (As believers, we shouldn't feel condemnation—and certainly not for struggling with sin.)

- stop condemning ourselves or others. (If God doesn't condemn us, then we shouldn't condemn ourselves or receive condemnation from others.) *But isn't it good to feel remorse?*
- stop trying to fight the flesh on our own. (Trying harder or using self-help techniques alone won't work.)
- lean into the Spirit of Christ who lives within each of us. (Paul says the Spirit gives us victory, and we can learn to live in the Spirit.)

Are there some other practical truths that stand out to you from today's reading (Romans 7:14–8:4)? If so, record them below:

We can overcome sin and follow God's way through His Spirit living in us.

How would you summarize the big idea for today?

God's gift of his son is all powerful over the sinful nature.

My friend Marybeth, who participated in the pilot group, summed it up this way, "Sinning stinks, but we're not condemned." However you phrased it, I hope you will walk away encouraged and prepared to fight whatever temptations or battles you face today. Remember, you have been set free from the power of sin!

Talk with God

Lord, I acknowledge that I struggle with sin. Help me to remember that You have set me free from the power of sin and have given me Your Spirit so that I can live in victory over sin. And help me to surrender all control to Your Holy Spirit who lives within me. Amen.

Memory Verse

Read the Memory Verse on page 76 several times, and then fill in the blanks below as you recite it:

And I am **convinced** that **nothing** can ever **separate** us from God's **love**. Neither **death** nor **life**, neither **angels** nor demons, neither our **fears** for **today** nor our **worries** about **tomorrow**—not even the **powers** of hell can **separate** us from God's love.

(Romans 8:38)

Big Idea

Though we still struggle with sin, God doesn't condemn us and gives us power through His Spirit to overcome sin.

DAY 4: SURRENDERING CONTROL

Extra Insight

The Greek word for law used in Romans is **nomos**. Sometimes law refers to the Torah in the Old Testament, but other times it seems to be defined more as "principle" or "rule" such as we find in Romans 7:21.[7]

With three children in college this year, my husband and I have been learning what it means to lose control. We have been transitioning from an authoritative role to more of an advisory role in their lives. This can be challenging because when they were small we controlled everything from when they went to bed to how many cookies they could eat. Now they can do what they want in terms of bedtimes and dessert and I'll never know!

Having control means getting to make decisions. I relished my young adult years when I could stay out late and eat an entire sleeve of Thin Mints when I felt like it! I wonder what you would love to control right now. Imagine getting to make decisions about the weather, other people, or even political elections. While that may sound nice, our ability to control our surroundings is limited. When it comes to our sinful nature, it can sometimes feel like trying to control the weather. We have to surrender control to a power much greater than ourselves.

Read Romans 8:5-8 and fill in the chart according to what is related to the flesh, or sinful nature, and what is associated with the Holy Spirit:

	Flesh / Sinful nature	Holy Spirit
Thinks about (v. 5)	*What nature desires*	*Spirit desires*
Leads to (v. 6)	*death*	*life & peace*
Posture toward God (vv. 7-8)	*hostile*	N/A (He is God)

When the Spirit of God is in control, we discover life and peace, and we please God. Yesterday we talked about the struggle with sin. We agree in our minds that we want to obey God, but we lack the power in our human strength. God in His mercy knew we couldn't find life, peace, and the ability to please Him without help. The Holy Spirit is the person of the Trinity (Father, Son, Holy Spirit) who dwells in us and enables us to live in the positive side of the contrasts above.

What are some words that come to your mind as you think about the Holy Spirit? *Peace, will, calm, support, strength*

Francis Chan has referred to this third person of the Trinity as the "Forgotten God." He says, "There is a big gap between what we read in Scripture about the Holy Spirit and how most believers and churches operate today."[8] I don't want to focus on the negative, but we must acknowledge that what we see in the lives of many believers and churches isn't always characterized by life, peace, and pleasing God. Chan's words move us to examine our own relationship with God's Holy Spirit. The Spirit, as Paul says in Romans 8, has the power to help us live new lives.

Read Romans 8:9-17 and list what you learn about the Holy Spirit from the following verses:

v. 9: *Has control of my life*

v. 10: *Body dead but spirit alive*

v. 11: *Will give life to our mortal bodies*

v. 13: *Will let us put aside our misdeeds*

v. 14: *Sons of God*

v. 15: *Gives us a spirit of sonship*

v. 16: *Testifies that we are children of God*

Take a moment to review these important truths by reading them aloud:

- The Holy Spirit lives in every person belonging to Christ. (v. 9)
- He gives us spiritual life. (v. 10)
- His power that raised Jesus from the dead is available to us. (v. 11)
- The Holy Spirit gives us the power to put to death the deeds of our sinful nature. (v. 13)
- Those who are led by the Holy Spirit are children of God. (v. 14)
- His Spirit doesn't make us fearful slaves. (v. 15)
- God adopted us as His children and uses the Holy Spirit to remind us that we belong to the Father. (vv. 15-16)

We definitely don't want to forget a God like this one! No wonder Jesus said in John 16:7, "But in fact, it is best for you that I go away, because if I don't, the

Advocate won't come. If I do go away, then I will send him to you." If left to my own reasoning, I would think it would be easier to live the Christian life if Jesus were physically present to help and guide me, but He said the Holy Spirit is better. And these verses show us why.

The kind of power we read about today is transformative, but does this power characterize our daily lives as followers of Jesus? Francis Chan said this, "Christ said it is better for us that the Spirit came, and I want to live like I know that is true. I don't want to keep crawling when I have the ability to fly."[9] Sometimes I live like a fearful slave instead of an adopted heir. I worry when my children struggle, and I have no control. I have awakened in the middle of the night or struggled to fall asleep because I am trying to figure out their friend, financial, and health struggles. When it comes to certain challenges in life, such as kids, health, and money, I can find myself crawling along in faith when I want to learn to trust the Holy Spirit and fly.

Based on the Scriptures we've read in Romans today, what changes would you like to see in your relationship with the Holy Spirit?

I need to give him more thought. He is the part of the trinity that I most often ignore.

Studying Romans gives us an opportunity to renew our minds as we realize the incredible power that we possess. This reminds me of the story of Ira Yates, a Texas rancher who traded his store for a huge parcel of land in Pecos County. The land was unfenced, with disputed boundaries, and known for seasons of drought. All of his friends advised him against the trade, but he did it anyway. The predictions seemed to be coming true when Yates was on the verge of bankruptcy, unable to pay the taxes on over 16,000 acres of land. As a last ditch effort, Yates allowed the Transcontinental Oil Company to drill on his land even though oil had never been found in West Texas west of the Pecos River. In 1926, the amount of oil found on his land made him an instant millionaire. It was a gusher that no one could have anticipated.[10]

Although Yates had been living in fear for years as his property threatened to bankrupt him, he had been a wealthy man all along. He just needed to drill down beneath the surface and allow his riches to come to the surface. In the same way, once we make a decision to follow Jesus, He gives us the gift of the Holy Spirit who lives inside of us. But He can become a forgotten God in our lives when we forget His presence and power. We are in danger of living as though we are spiritually poor when we possess great spiritual treasure. We must drill down beneath the surface and yield every part of our lives to Him.

Even if those around us think we are crazy or don't see the value in surrendering control, we can choose to believe what God says about the gift of His Spirit.

This yielding can be a mysterious thing at times. I wish I could offer you "five steps to surrendering control to the Holy Spirit," since I am a big fan of working through step-by-step instructions. However, walking with God isn't a checklist but a personal relationship. The Holy Spirit is not an "it" or a magical "force" as in *Star Wars*. He is a person, and the Scriptures tell us we are capable of bringing Him grief by the way we live (Ephesians 4:30). We talk to Him and listen as He speaks to us; He provides spiritual gifts, comfort, and understanding.

At times I can sense His presence helping me do things I never thought possible. Other times, I feel nothing and must believe by faith that He is near— as close as my breath. Romans 8:12 says that we are no longer under obligation to do what our sinful natures urge us to do. We are not animals governed by uncontrollable passions. God has taken up residence inside of us and enables us to put to death the deeds of the flesh or sinful nature by the power of the Holy Spirit.

What practical wisdom can you share related to allowing the Holy Spirit to guide our actions and decisions? What helps you give the Spirit control so that you don't give in to the flesh or sinful nature?

As I think about Ira Yates drilling down, I recognize that yielding to the Spirit is an internal experience that takes place in our hearts and minds. Just last night I got into a silly argument with my husband about directions to a destination. He said something that rubbed me the wrong way, and I felt an internal battle. I wanted to speak unkindly and lacked the power of self-control, so I asked God to help me. I admitted that I couldn't restrain my tongue on my own, and the Holy Spirit gave me the power to be quiet.

Asking for the Holy Spirit's help in prayer is where I usually start in my quest to surrender control. Another thing that helps me yield to God when my flesh wants to be in charge is to recall Scriptures that I have read or memorized. Someone once told me that memorizing Scripture is like increasing the Holy Spirit's vocabulary in your life. (You may be doing that with your Romans memory work!) Other times when I sense the war between my flesh or sinful nature and my desire to yield to the Holy Spirit, I will call a Christian friend and ask for prayer. I find this especially helpful when I am trying to overcome a sinful habit. These are just a few things that come to mind.

Walking with God isn't a checklist but a personal relationship.

Allowing the Spirit to have control in our lives isn't a formulaic method but a personal relationship. My prayer is that you would drill down deep and develop closeness with the Holy Spirit of God who lives within you. Give Him authority to make decisions so that He is much more than an advisor who makes a suggestion. Together let's seek to yield and live in sync with the Holy Spirit so that we can experience life and peace and live in a way that pleases God. This is good news for daily life!

Talk with God

Holy Spirit, I yield control of my life to You. I need Your power and wisdom. I struggle with giving in to the flesh. Help me to remember that I am not under obligation to my flesh. You live inside of me. You enable me with the same power that raised Jesus from the grave. You have not given me a spirit of fear but the assurance that I belong to the Father. Help my life to reflect these truths. Amen.

Memory Verse Exercise

Read the Memory Verse on page 76 several times, and then fill in the blanks below as you recite it:

And I am __convinced__ that __nothing__ can ever __separate__ us __from__ __God's__ __love__. Neither __death__ nor __life__, neither __demons__ nor __angels__, neither __our__ __fears__ for __today__ nor our __worries__ about __tomorrow__. Not even the __powers__ of __hell__ can __separate__ us from __God's__ __love__.

(**Romans 8:38**)

Big Idea

We don't have to do what the flesh or sinful nature demands; we can surrender control to the Holy Spirit, which leads to life and peace and pleasing God.

DAY 5: FUTURE GLORY

Scripture Focus

Romans 8:18-39

We have covered some gospel ground this week in Romans 6–8 as we've heard the good news about daily life. Paul wrote about freedom from the law, the dangers of legalism, our continual struggle with sin, and the power of the Holy Spirit. Now we come to one of my very favorite portions of his Letter to the Romans. (You might hear me say that a few more times in our study because there is so much good stuff here!)

So many incredible truths for daily living jump off the pages of Romans 8, but we are going to focus on three found in verses 18-39:

- Life is messy in the here and now, but we look forward to an incredible future.
- God works even the messy parts of life together for good for those who love Him.
- Circumstantial ease is not our measuring rod for God's love for us.

We left off yesterday with Paul telling the church in Rome that they were not fearful slaves but heirs of God's glory. In Romans 8:17 he said, "But if we are to share his glory, we must also share his suffering." If I could sit down with you over a cup of tea, I know you might share some things you are celebrating but also some stories of suffering.

Write one or two challenges you have faced or are facing that have been difficult: *death of parents* *health struggles* *Mom's illness*

Whether it is physical, mental, emotional, or spiritual, we all suffer because we live in a fallen world. Dealing with my daughter's alopecia, moving, seeing kids off to college, and having a busy schedule of traveling and writing have been my challenges recently. That may sound like a walk in the park compared to what you are going through right now. Let's validate each other's struggles rather than stack them up against each other. People used to think my daughter with alopecia had cancer when she was completely bald. One day she confided to me that she felt guilty for struggling so much with alopecia, especially when compared with cancer. I reminded her that her pain was legitimate and she shouldn't compare.

We can't minimize our problems because others seem to have "worse" ones. The good news is that Jesus can relate to each one of us. He suffered in every way and died to bring us back into relationship with the Father. When we feel pain, we can identify with Him and take comfort that He understands.

The good news about suffering is that it has an expiration date. This brings us to our first key concept today.

1. Life is messy in the here and now, but we look forward to an incredible future.

Read Romans 8:18-25 which follows, and then match each beginning to its proper ending by writing the correct letter in the blank:

[18]Yet what we suffer now is nothing compared to the glory he will reveal to us later. [19]For all creation is waiting eagerly for that future day when God will reveal who his children really are. [20]Against its will,

all creation was subjected to God's curse. But with eager hope, ²¹the creation looks forward to the day when it will join God's children in glorious freedom from death and decay. ²²For we know that all creation has been groaning as in the pains of childbirth right up to the present time. ²³And we believers also groan, even though we have the Holy Spirit within us as a foretaste of future glory, for we long for our bodies to be released from sin and suffering. We, too, wait with eager hope for the day when God will give us our full rights as his adopted children, including the new bodies he has promised us. ²⁴We were given this hope when we were saved. (If we already have something, we don't need to hope for it. ²⁵But if we look forward to something we don't yet have, we must wait patiently and confidently.)

__F__ 1. What we suffer now

__D__ 2. All creation is waiting for the day when

__H__ 3. All creation was subjected to

__A__ 4. Creation looks forward to

__B__ 5. All creation has been groaning

__G__ 6. We have the Holy Spirit as a

__C__ 7. We long for our bodies to be

__E__ 8. We wait with eager hope for when

A. the day when it will join God's children in glorious freedom from death and decay.

B. as in the pains of childbirth.

C. released from sin and suffering.

D. God will reveal who His children really are.

E. God will give us our full rights as children including new bodies.

F. is nothing compared to the glory He will reveal later.

G. foretaste of future glory.

H. God's curse.

With a matching exercise we can be so focused on finding the right answers that we don't take in the meaning. Go back and read the statements slowly. What stands out to you as you read about the future glory God has planned?

How perfect it will be

When I read these verses, I thought about labor. I was incredibly blessed to have four children with only three labors. (Twins!) Labor was no picnic, but it seems like a distant memory now. I don't think about it much when I look at my kids. It was a short, agonizing time. So when I hear Paul talk about this life as labor, it gives me a whole new perspective on the daily challenges I face.

Whether or not you have given birth, what are some adjectives you would use to describe labor?

My words are *intense*, *painful*, and *short* (at least in the grand scheme of life). Suffering isn't fun, but it is fleeting for the believer in Christ. We are going to look back on this life as labor. The rest of eternity will be filled with glory and removed from the very presence of sin.

How do these truths affect your posture toward your current struggles today? *We have to remember that that glorious day is coming*

Knowing the suffering of this life will be over one day can help us get through it.

When reading this passage, I also took note that we will be given new bodies. Anyone else want to say "Amen"? Whether you have a chronic health problem or just aren't fond of wrinkles and cellulite, it's nice to know this body isn't forever. Thinking about future glory gives us perspective, but I love that Paul doesn't leave it there. Though suffering isn't forever, it is for today. So God gives us hope and help until we get to heaven.

Read Romans 8:26-30 and summarize the example Paul gives of how the Holy Spirit helps us in our weakness:
He groans for us – beyond words

Once again Paul reminds the church of the work of the Holy Spirit, who helps us in our weakness in many ways. One example Paul gives is prayer. When we don't know what to pray, we can ask the Holy Spirit to take over. This goes along with surrendering control, which we studied yesterday. In order to surrender fully, we must believe that God will do it better than we could. This brings us to our second key concept.

2. God works even the messy parts of life together for good for those who love Him.

As you read Romans 8:26-30, did you notice a verse that you may have seen before? Romans 8:28 says, "And we know that God causes everything to work together for the good of those who love God and are called according to his purpose for them."

How do these words encourage or confuse you as you seek to reconcile your reality with this truth?

Sometimes it feels like there's no way to understand and we must have faith that he knows best

We must use caution in sharing these words when others are experiencing times of grief or suffering, because we all need time to process our emotions. Paul's words are not meant to be a trite saying we use to tell people not to be sad in their suffering. What these verses can do is give us a bigger picture of how the good and bad in this life can be used of God. Think of Christ. The cross didn't feel good in the moment, but God worked Christ's suffering to bring good for all people through His sacrifice.

I had the privilege of sitting with a dear friend in the final stages of his life and writing his memoir. My friend, who was my age and dying of brain cancer, wanted me to title the book "All Things" in reference to Romans 8:28. In the midst of his suffering, he shared with me that he was a winner no matter what happened. He said that if he was healed in this life, then he would get to spend more time with his family and serving God; and if he went to heaven, he would suffer no more. He understood some of the key words in this verse. It is not some things but all things that can work together for good when we love God and are called according to His purpose. Even health problems, relationship strains, and financial difficulties can work together to produce strong character, opportunities to share God's love, and reminders of the hope of a future in heaven.

Our greatest trials can be transformed into our greatest triumphs as we allow God to work things together for good.

Have you been able to see something challenging work together for good in your life? If so, write about it here:

Our greatest trials can be transformed into our greatest triumphs as we allow God to work things together for good.

I've seen the Lord use my daughter's alopecia to grow her in so many ways. She has developed compassion for others who are hurting. In fact, she is studying missions in college because she found hope in Christ through her pain and wants others to know Him too. It hasn't always been easy or made sense, but we have had just a few glimpses of how God is working all things together and bringing good from it.

We could say so much more about this concept of God working all things for good, but I want us to have time for our final verses, which are so encouraging for daily life. This brings us to our third key concept.

3. Circumstantial ease is not our measuring rod for God's love for us.

Read Romans 8:31-39 and record below any words or phrases that stand out to you:

Shall trouble or hardship... - Neither...nor

Write your name in the blanks to bring these truths a little closer to home:

God is for *Georgia* —who can be against *Georgia* ?

He didn't spare His only Son, so He won't withhold anything else from *Georgia* .

God has given *Georgia* right standing with Himself.

Christ Jesus died for *Georgia* and is sitting at God's right hand pleading for *Georgia* .

Nothing can separate us from God's love. He didn't spare even His own Son. None of these powerful forces can stand up against God's great love for us:

- Death nor life
- Angels nor demons
- Fears for today nor worries for tomorrow
- Not even the powers of hell
- No power in the sky above or in the earth below
- Nothing in all creation

The chapter ends with Paul saying that nothing ever will be able to separate us from the love of God that is revealed in Christ Jesus our Lord. Even if it feels like one bad thing after another is happening. Even if life isn't turning out the way we thought it would. Even if we don't feel it. God loves us.

We need to be careful not to think God shows us love only when something good happens, because then when calamity strikes, we will be tempted to doubt His love. We were so excited when my daughter's hair began to grow back in her senior year of high school. We talked about God's love and grace. But over time, her hair has been in a continual process of falling out and coming back. It is a rollercoaster at times. Yet God's love isn't rising and falling with that ride. His love is constant—when He heals and when He doesn't, when we are in a sweet season or a difficult one, when hair is falling out and coming in. His love never changes.

I don't know if it is easy or difficult for you to embrace God's love today. I pray that by faith you will believe this good news about His love whether you are feeling it or not, remembering that:

- Life is messy in the here and now, but we look forward to an incredible future.
- God works even the messy parts of life together for good for those who love Him.
- Circumstantial ease is not our measuring rod for God's love for us.

Put a star by the concept above that resonates most strongly in your life today.

Above all, remember that we have good news for daily life because we have a God who promises us overwhelming victory through Christ!

Talk with God

Abba, Father, I am overwhelmed by Your love. Thank You for reminding me that this life is like labor—intense but short. I'm looking forward to a new body and new home in heaven. Thank You for your Holy Spirit who helps me in my weakness. Help me trust You even when I can't make sense of my circumstances and hold tight to the truth that nothing can separate me from You. Amen.

Memory Verse Exercise

Read the Memory Verse on page 76 several times, and then fill in the blanks on the following page as you recite it:

Big Idea

The hope of heaven, the Holy Spirit, and the love of God provide good news to help us navigate the daily struggles of life.

And I am _certain_ that _nothing_ can ~~ever~~ ever _separate_ us _from_ ~~the God's~~ God's love. _Neither_ _death_ nor _life_, _neither_ _angels_ nor _demons_. ~~Neither~~ our _fears_ for _today_ our _worries_ about _tomorrow_ — _not_ even the _powers_ of _hell_ can _separate_ _us_ from _God's love_.

(Romans 8:38)

Weekly Wrap Up

Review the Big Idea for each day, and then write any personal application that comes to mind.

Day 1: Independence Day
Big Idea: God has given us power over sin and calls us to walk daily in that truth by faith.

Personal Application:_____

_____

Day 2: The Failure of Legalism
Big Idea: We need a clear understanding of the purpose of God's law so that we don't veer to the side of legalism or license as we follow Jesus daily.

Personal Application:_____

_____

Day 3: Struggling but Not Condemned
Big Idea: Though we still struggle with sin, God doesn't condemn us and gives us power through His Spirit to overcome sin.

Personal Application:_____

_____

Day 4: Surrendering Control
Big Idea: We don't have to do what the flesh or sinful nature demands; we can surrender control to the Holy Spirit, which leads to life and peace and pleasing God.

Personal Application:_____

_____

Day 5: Future Glory
Big Idea: The hope of heaven, the Holy Spirit, and the love of God provide good news to help us navigate the daily struggles of life.

Personal Application:_____

_____

VIDEO VIEWER GUIDE: WEEK 3

GOOD NEWS ABOUT DAILY LIFE

Romans 6:12-16

It's easy to confuse the presence of _____ with the absence of _____.

John 15:14-15

The _____ is real.

Romans 7:14-25

Philippians 3:12-14

We can't be _____ without _____.

Romans 8:1-5, 11

God's promises give us _____ on the journey.

Romans 8:17

Romans 8:31-39

Week 4

Good News About God's Plan

Romans 9–11

Memory Verse

⁹If you openly declare that Jesus is Lord and believe in your heart that God raised him from the dead, you will be saved. ¹⁰For it is by believing in your heart that you are made right with God, and it is by openly declaring your faith that you are saved.

(Romans 10:9-10)

DAY 1: OVERLAPPING TRUTHS

Scripture Focus

Romans 9

Have you ever looked at a picture that was zoomed in so close you couldn't identify what it was? Then when you zoomed out, you could see the object with greater context. This week we'll find Paul widening his scope as he teaches about God's plan.

So far we've seen the good news about faith, hope, and daily living in Romans 1–8. Paul's discourse takes a sharp turn in chapters 9–11 with historical review and many references from the Hebrew Scriptures. It seems that Paul could have gone straight from chapter 8 to chapter 12 with better continuity. I heard someone joke that for these three chapters Paul pulled an old sermon out of his bottom dresser drawer to beef up the letter's word count. However, we know if Paul took the time to review the past in light of God's plan, he had good reasons.

Paul wanted to help the church in Rome understand God's plan of grace that includes Gentiles against the backdrop of the spiritual heritage of God's relationship with Israel. Like zooming out to include more in a picture, Paul reviewed the larger picture of how God has interacted with His people throughout history. He made it clear that it is faith rather than ancestry that God has always valued by retelling the narrative of Abraham, Isaac, Jacob, and Moses—a narrative that every Jew would have known. He also made connections to this plan for the Gentiles. In making the point of what constitutes a true Jew, Paul touched on some controversial doctrines. In fact, discussing the content of Romans 9 led to the first argument I ever had with my husband!

Sean and I were both Bible theology majors when we were dating. Somehow we got into a conversation about divine sovereignty and human responsibility. In other words, we disagreed about whether we choose God or God chooses us. As I look back on it, I realize we actually were saying the same things using different words. So many times that can happen, especially when it comes to trying to make sense of overlapping truths.

Overlapping truths are when two opposite statements are simultaneously true. For example, when we try to define how Jesus was fully human and also fully God, our words fall short. In the same way, defining exactly where and how God's sovereignty and our human responsibility overlap can feel like nailing Jell-O to a wall. The last thing I want to start is a war over words reminiscent of my first fight with my husband.

In that spirit, let's read these verses with curiosity and context.

Digging Deeper

The explanation of salvation in Romans has sometimes been referred to as the Romans Road. For a clear explanation of the essence of the good news found in Romans, check out the Digging Deeper article for Week 4, "The Romans Road" (see AbingdonWomen .com/Romans).

Read Romans 9:1-5 and write below what lengths Paul said he would go to so that Jews would be saved. (v. 3)

He would be cursed & cut off from Christ

Here Paul wanted to make it clear that *God has blessed the Jews*. As the apostle to the Gentiles, he took time in Romans 9–11 to give a lot of backstory to illustrate how the Jews are a part of God's plan and how that plan came to fruition in Christ. Paul might have gone to great lengths to remind the church of its Jewish roots because Rome had a long history of anti-Jewish sentiment.[2] Jews had recently been able to return after being expelled from Rome, and Paul may have been addressing the culture's influence on the church.

Paul said in regard to the nation of Israel that God clearly had:

- chosen them as adopted children
- revealed glory to them
- made covenants with them
- given them the law
- given them the privilege of worship and of receiving promises

Paul went on to point out that the patriarchs as well as Christ Himself were Israelites. So we can be sure that God's hand of blessing is on the Jewish people.

In the next section, Paul explained that the Jews were not the only people included in God's plan. His blessing isn't based on who your parents or grandparents are or are not. The Lord is sovereign and not bound by family trees.

Read Romans 9:6-29 and write below any insights that stand out to you or questions you may have:

We are all powerless and saved only because he chose to do so. How does evangelism fit?

What do you think is the main point Paul is trying to make in this discourse?

By reading the full context, we see that Paul's overarching point is that God does not call people based on their family relations. Gentiles are included because God says they will be. We cannot ignore the intensity with which Paul highlights the sovereignty of God, which raises a question that has been debated through the ages: Do we choose to follow God, or does God predetermine who will follow Him?

Let's take a moment to consider two primary theological camps on this subject. Calvinism is a term used to refer to the teachings of John Calvin, who emphasized the supremacy of God in choosing us. The acronym TULIP is often used to explain the doctrines of pure Calvinism. Here are its basic tenets with my own brief explanations:

	Explanation
T – Total Depravity	Every person is born a sinner and cannot be saved without God's help. This idea is sometimes referred to as original sin. (Most Christians would agree with some doctrine of original sin.)
U – Unconditional Election	God saves people not based on their choices but on the intention of His will.
L – Limited Atonement	Christ's death on the cross was effective and saving not for everyone but for those who were chosen.
I – Irresistible Grace	Those whom God has chosen for salvation will not be able to resist His pursuit of them.
P – Perseverance of the Saints	Those who are chosen cannot lose their salvation.

Those in this camp do not necessarily hold to every one of these five points, but generally they focus on God's predetermination (preselection) of those who become believers. Traditionally, Presbyterian, Lutheran, and Reformed denominations have leaned in this direction.

On the other side of the argument is Arminian theology, named for the Dutch Reformed theologian Jacobus Arminius. Arminians focus on the free will of each person to choose God. Though there is no acronym, such as TULIP, there are Five Articles of Remonstrance that were written in response to the Calvinist view. These articles correspond to tenets of TULIP but not in the same order:

I. Conditional Election	Those who choose to believe in Christ will be saved. (Corresponds to Unconditional Election in TULIP.)

2. Unlimited Atonement	Christ died for every person, so atonement is not limited. (Corresponds to Limited Atonement in TULIP.)
3. Deprivation	People cannot be saved on their own (original sin), but with the help of Christ and the Holy Spirit they can be transformed. (Corresponds to Total Depravity in TULIP.)
4. Resistible Grace	People can reject God's pursuit by their free will. (Corresponds to Irresistible Grace in TULIP.)
5. Assurance and Security	Believers can feel assured of their salvation, but the possibility that salvation can be lost if the person chooses to reject God cannot be ruled out. (Corresponds to Perseverance of the Saints in TULIP.)[4]

Extra Insight

In Romans 9:25-26, Paul quotes the prophet Hosea (1:10 and 2:23), who prophesied about the inclusion of the Gentiles over seven hundred years before Christ was born.

Those in this camp may or may not hold to every one of these articles but generally highlight the choice of each person to follow or reject God. Historically, Baptist, Methodist, and Wesleyan denominations were influenced by Arminian thought.

I respect many people—including pastors, teachers, and theologians—who hold opposing views in regard to predestination and free will. If this topic interests you, I would encourage you to investigate it further. I actually find myself seeing these views as cooperating rather than competing. You might call me a Cal-minian, because I see it this way:

God chooses us.	Jesus replied, "…No one can come to me unless the Father who sent me draws them to me, and at the last day I will raise them up."
	(John 6:43-44)
We choose God.	"Everyone who calls on the name of the LORD will be saved."
	(Romans 10:13)

In my marriage, I don't question whether Sean chose me or I chose Him. We chose each other. When it comes to our salvation, I cannot define exactly where divine sovereignty and human responsibility intertwine, but I believe they are both true according to Scripture. Jesus said, "Look! I stand at the door and knock. If you hear my voice and open the door, I will come in, and we will share a meal together as friends" (Revelation 3:20). I believe Jesus knocks on every person's door, but we have to answer.

Having *very briefly* discussed Calvinism and Arminianism, what are your thoughts on the issue of predestination and free will? Write

a brief statement of your personal view, or if you prefer, record whatever questions you may have.

I struggle w/ the idea that some are not chosen and how that intersects w/ evangelism & missions

Many great theologians over the course of history have struggled with these lofty concepts, so don't feel discouraged if, like me, you don't identify with a clearly decided view. God reminds us through Paul in Romans 9 that He is the potter and we are the clay. His ways are higher than our limited understandings (Isaiah 55:8-9). Even though we've spent some time looking at Calvinism and Arminianism, I don't want us to miss the greater context of why Paul raised the topic.

Using references from the Hebrew Scriptures, Paul demonstrated to his audience that God didn't change the divine plan by bringing Gentiles into the church. Rather, God fulfilled the plan He had in place all along. God's purposes will prevail, and we can either fight against them or choose to trust Him when we don't understand our circumstances or the Scriptures we encounter.

Discussing the theological topics that Romans 9 brings to the surface is good, but the issue of divine sovereignty and human responsibility is not the main point that the apostle Paul is making in this section of his letter.

Read Romans 9:30-33 and fill in the blanks:

Following the _____*law*_____ won't save anyone.

_____*faith*_____ in God is how we get right with Him.

While we can debate many sections of Romans 9 and agree to disagree on which theological camp we lean toward when it comes to predestination and free will, we can all come together in trusting God.

Paul highlights that God has blessed the Israelites and points out that God doesn't save people based on their birth or behavior.[5] God invites us to get right with Him through faith, reminding us not to stumble over the law. We will never be disgraced when we trust in Him.

I pray we won't let our differing opinions on any nonessential theological distinctive to become a rock that makes us fall. Christ himself became a stumbling block, so we know that anything can trip us up if we aren't careful—including our discussion of history or theology.

As we end today, would you consider if any stumbling blocks might be keeping you from trusting God more? If something comes to mind, write it in the margin:

> God's purposes will prevail, and we can either fight against them or choose to trust Him when we don't understand our circumstances or the Scriptures we encounter.

Some of my recent stumbling blocks include trying to please people, doubting myself, and worrying about the future. These things don't help me trust God. I'm asking God to help me recognize and address them so I won't trip as I run the race of faith. The Lord knows our tendency to stumble over rules, laws, and opinions. Let's ask Him to show us today how we can trust Him more so that we can yield to His plan rather than overthink it.

Talk with God

Lord, I love Your Word. I want to know You more. Help me not to miss the forest for the trees as I read Romans in context. You are sovereign, and You've given us choices to make. Grow my understanding of how these truths intertwine so that I can trust You more. Amen.

Big Idea

God blesses and calls His people and invites us to trust His plan.

Memory Verse Exercise

Read the Memory Verse on page 106 several times, and then fill in the blanks below as you recite it:

⁹If you openly *declare that Jesus is* Lord *and believe in your* heart *that God raised him from the* dead*, you will be* saved*. ¹⁰For it is by believing in your heart that you are made right with God, and it is by openly declaring your faith that you are saved.*

(Romans 10:9-10)

DAY 2: RELATIONSHIPS OVER RULES

Scripture Focus

Romans 10:1-13

I grew up in a small town in East Texas. I had an older brother and sister as well as a younger sister. I fell into that middle child position of wanting to keep the peace. I tried to follow the rules at home and at school. I heard the stories of the Bible in Sunday school and at summer camps and vacation Bible schools. The message I received from all my spiritual exposure was that I should try to be good. I'm not sure if it was the way the messages were taught or my own filtering of the teaching through my birth order and personality type—the way I am wired.

In the little church my family attended, we took Communion every week. In fact, our family often stayed after church to wash the tiny glass cups that

were passed in a shiny gold tray each week. Children were not allowed to take one of the little pieces of bread or small glasses of grape juice until they had made a personal decision to follow Jesus and had professed it publicly by being baptized.

I had not been baptized because I thought that deciding to follow Jesus meant you would always be good and never do bad things again. My sins were quiet and behind the scenes but very real to me. I teased my sister, hid things under the bed instead of putting them away, and didn't always obey my parents.

One day I saw my older brother and sister fighting outside in the front yard. I stood at the screen door and watched them scream at each other in front of the watching world. I stood there thinking, "And they drink the grape juice at church!" I didn't know the word *hypocrite*, but I was judging them in my thoughts. I determined then not to make a formal decision and get baptized until I would never be bad again.

I misunderstood the gospel at that time. It wasn't until a few years later when a Sunday school teacher explained that following Jesus doesn't mean I would never sin. She said being a Christian isn't about being good; it is about being forgiven through the blood of Christ.

As we come to Romans 10, we find one of the clearest explanations of why my early belief system of "doing good" isn't God's way.

Read Romans 10:1-4 and answer the following questions:

Whom does Paul wish would be saved? (v. 1)

The Israelites

How does he describe their enthusiasm for God? (v. 2)

They are zealous

How does he say the Jews got off course in their pursuit of God? (v. 3)

They tried to establish their own righteousness

What did Christ do in regard to the law? (v. 4)

He put an end to it for those who believe

The law was never meant to be a permanent fixture. In a letter to the Galatian church, Paul said, "Let me put it another way. The law was our guardian until Christ came; it protected us until we could be made right with God through faith" (Galatians 3:24).

The Israelites were looking for the Messiah, but somehow many of them lost the awareness of their need for a Savior and began to trust in a set of rules and

regulations to save them. Paul indicates that the Jews in Rome who believed in Christ had fallen back into following the law when Christ had fulfilled its purpose. Old habits die hard.

Have you had a season in your life when you focused on following a set of rules? If anything comes to mind, write it below:

Trying to follow a specific diet

Today I still can find myself fighting the desire to earn God's favor by following rules. I may not hold to the strict laws of the Old Testament, but sometimes I inwardly set standards for myself and then feel shame when I fail to complete them. Do you ever struggle in this way? Whether or not you are wired like me, we will find good news that has the power to change everything in today's reading.

Read Romans 10:5-8, and circle the correct answer for each statement:

1. Moses wrote that the law's way of making us right with God is

    A. Obedience to some of its commands

    B. Obedience to all of its commands

    C. You don't really have to follow much of it

2. Faith's way of getting right with God says

    A. "Who will go down to the place of the dead and bring Christ back to life?"

    B. "Who will go up to heaven to bring Christ down to earth?"

    C. "The message is very close at hand; it is on your lips and in your heart."

Paul quotes Deuteronomy 30:12-14 in this part of Romans, reminding the people again that God's plan isn't a new one; it is a fulfillment of the original one. In the next verses in Deuteronomy 30, we see that Moses gave the Israelites a powerful picture of God's desire for His people:

15"Now listen! Today I am giving you a choice between life and death, between prosperity and disaster. 16For I command you this day to love the LORD your God and to keep his commands, decrees, and regulations by walking in his ways. If you

Answers: 1. B 2. C

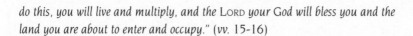

do this, you will live and multiply, and the LORD *your God will bless you and the land you are about to enter and occupy." (vv. 15-16)*

Moses went on to express God's heart when he said, "Oh, that you would choose life, so that you and your descendants might live!" (Deuteronomy 30:19b). Obeying God's commands was to be preceded by loving God. Following God's law was supposed to spring out of loving Him and walking with Him. The Israelites got off course whenever they put rules before relationship. When enforcing laws took precedence over their commitment to love, they were blinded, ultimately causing many to miss the Messiah.

In the same way, as followers of Christ we must guard against overcomplicating the simple gospel message. Paul lays it out clearly in our memory verse for this week.

Read Romans 10:9-10 in the margin, and underline the verbs used to describe our actions. How would you summarize these verses in your own words?

If you share that Jesus is lord and was believe in the resurrection, God will save you

Two key verbs stand out. We *confess* with our mouths (the New Living Translation uses *declare*), and we *believe* in our hearts. The Greek word for "confess" is *homologeo*. It means "to profess; to declare openly, speak out freely; to profess one's self the worshipper of one."[6]

"Believe" in Greek is *pisteuo* and means "to think to be true, to be persuaded of, to credit, place confidence in."[7] It is used more than fifteen times in the letter to the Romans!

Look again at Romans 10:8 (in the margin), which is a quote from Deuteronomy 30:14. Where is this message that is so close at hand?

One your lips & in your heart

Paul links the idea from Deuteronomy of having God's message on the lips and in the heart with the concept of confessing Jesus is Lord with our mouths and believing in our hearts that God raised Him from the dead. He is again connecting to familiar Scriptures to bridge contexts and help his readers understand that God's plan has always been about faith, not law.

When my Sunday school teacher explained the gospel to me, I found it to be good news. I realized that I didn't have to keep striving and failing; the only way for me to get right with God was through faith in Christ. We declare with

[9]If you confess with your mouth that Jesus is Lord and believe in your heart that God raised him from the dead, you will be saved. [10]For with the heart one believes and is justified, and with the mouth one confesses and is saved. (Romans 10:9-10 ESV)

"The message is very close at hand; it is on your lips and in your heart." (Romans 10:8)

our mouths and believe in our hearts the good news about Christ, and then we are saved.

This salvation is threefold, as we talked about last week:

- We are saved from the penalty of sin immediately, which is justification.
- We are being saved from the power of sin as we grow in faith, which is sanctification.
- We will be saved from the presence of sin when we go to heaven, which is glorification.

I don't know whether or not you have personally confessed with your mouth and believed in your heart this good news that changes everything. If you aren't sure, you can be sure this very minute. You can say with your mouth and believe in your heart that:

God loves you.
For this is how God loved the world: He gave his one and only Son, so that everyone who believes in him will not perish but have eternal life. (John 3:16)

You are a sinner.
For everyone has sinned; we all fall short of God's glorious standard.
(Romans 3:23)

Christ died for your sin.
But God showed his great love for us by sending Christ to die for us while we were still sinners.
(Romans 5:8)

You want to receive Christ.
But to all who believed in him and accepted him, he gave the right to become children of God.
(John 1:12)

Once we have done this, we can be assured of this salvation we are talking about.

I remember a time in high school, many years after I had made this commitment, when I began to doubt whether I was truly saved because my childhood memories of my decision were fuzzy. Everyone around me assumed I was because I had been baptized and had talked about Jesus. One night a youth leader was teaching Romans 10 in youth group. She said that if we weren't sure about our salvation, we shouldn't wonder. We could settle it in our hearts and minds and be sure. It was like she was reading my mind. I wrote my declaration

of belief in Christ in my journal that night so that going forward I wouldn't struggle with fear or uncertainty related to my position before God—my identity.

Looking back now, I believe my original decision was the beginning of my faith walk, but I sure am thankful for that leader who spared me years of more internal questioning. I hope you can rest assured tonight when you put your head on the pillow that your salvation is sure.

Read Romans 10:11-13 and note who verse 13 says will be saved:

Everyone who calls on him

Everyone who calls on God will be saved. God is sovereign, but He offers everyone the opportunity to call on His name. Now that's good news!

As we end our time today, I invite you to take some time to reflect on your personal salvation story. It may not fit neatly into a box and may be more of a present reality than a past experience. Even so, I encourage you to make an effort to answer the following questions. (If you aren't sure and can't answer some of them, it is okay to leave them blank.)

What are some misconceptions you had about God before you understood the gospel message, which we read today?

Who was influential in helping you gain clarity about the meaning of Christ's death and resurrection?

The pastor (& his wife) of my first church

If you have confessed with your mouth and believed in your heart that Jesus Christ is Lord, briefly describe that experience. Feel free to be as specific or as general as you wish.

Don't completely remember but I do remember the baptism

Our faith is much more about relationship than following rules.

Have you ever doubted and/or reaffirmed your decision at a later time? If so, tell about that briefly:

Revisiting our personal stories of faith can help us trace God's hand in drawing us toward Him. It also helps us remember that our faith is much more about relationship than following rules. I pray that as we study Romans together our relationships with Christ continue to grow as we encounter again the good news that has the power to change everything!

Talk with God

Lord, I am grateful that You made a way for us to come to You through faith. Help me to remember Your sacrifice in sending Your one and only Son to die for us. Thank You for the salvation that I have through the cross. Show me what it means to declare and believe this message so that others can also know Your love. Amen.

Big Idea

We are not saved by the law but by declaring with our mouths and believing in our hearts the good news about Christ.

Memory Verse Exercise

Read the Memory Verse on page 106 several times, and then fill in the blanks below as you recite it:

⁹If you _openly_ declare that Jesus is _Lord_ and believe in your _heart_ that God raised him from the _grave_, you will be _saved_ ¹⁰For it is by _believing_ in your _heart_ that you are made right with God, and it is by _openly_ declaring your _faith_ that you are saved.

(Romans 10:9-10)

DAY 3: BEAUTIFUL FEET

Scripture Focus

Romans 10:14-21

Are you a shoe girl—someone who loves shoes? My closet used to consist of varying shades of black and brown practical footwear. But in recent years, I've enjoyed more diversity in the color and style of my shoes based on where I'm going and what I'm doing. Today in Romans 10 we will find Paul talking about beautiful feet!

Since we're talking about feet today, take a moment and write down your current favorite personal footwear:

Sugar skull Chuck Taylors

Gladys Aylward - Missionary

Actually, Paul's good news about feet isn't referencing shoes at all but the people who share God's message. So far this week we've focused on the good news about God's plan. We've seen that Paul took extra care to be sure that the Jews and Gentiles in the church in Rome understood their common ground in Christ. He wanted Jewish believers to see the flaw in focusing on observance of the law for salvation and to understand that all are saved by faith, not by family tree. At the same time, he showed that God's plan had been entrusted to the Jewish nation. The Gentiles needed to understand the history of God's sovereign plan in order to understand and appropriate Christ's sacrifice.

Chapters 9–11 of Romans are loaded with references from the Hebrew Scriptures, which is now much of our Old Testament. As one source points out, "A rough count finds twenty-four quotations in Romans 9–11. When we consider that there are about eighty quotations in all Paul's letters, this figure is remarkable. In other words, 30 percent of Paul's Old Testament quotations are in these three chapters."[8] We can't miss Paul's intent in using these Scriptures so that both Jews and Gentiles understood that they are united in Christ.

On a related note, I pray that our study of Romans will encourage you to dig into the Old Testament. Paul referenced Abraham, Moses, David, and many other foundational characters and stories in order to help his audience build theological connections to Christ. My hope is that studying Romans will encourage us to keep seeking God's plan in our own lives as we take time to study God's plan throughout history.

We've seen that in communicating God's plan, Paul clearly stated that each person must confess with their mouth that Jesus is Lord and believe in their heart that God raised Him from the dead (Romans 10:8-9). Now he will explain how that message reaches those who haven't heard the good news that changes everything.

Read Romans 10:14-15 and fill in the following blanks using your own words based on what you read. (If possible, you may find it helpful to use the New Living Translation or refer to several translations.)

How can they *call on / ask* unless they *believe* ?

How can they ___belive___ if they
___haven't heard___?

How can they ___hear___ unless someone
___tells them___?

How will anyone ___preach___ unless they
___are sent___?

Paul ends this progression with a quotation from the prophet Isaiah: "How beautiful are the feet of messengers who bring good news!" (Romans 10:15; see also Isaiah 52:7). Remember, this isn't about the shoes in our closets or even the physical beauty of our feet. Anyone who brings the truth about God to others has beautiful feet. As you look at this progression, I wonder how it connects with your faith story.

Has anyone ever invited you to church, Bible study, or some other gathering that led you to grow in faith? If so, name them here:

Stephanie / pastor

Who has initiated spiritual conversations with you?

Though we can encounter Christ's message in books and on radio, television, podcasts, and the internet, most of us have a more personal story of encountering this message through people in our lives—people with beautiful feet, as Paul says.

If we were to brainstorm ways to have beautiful feet, a great place to start would be to consider how the message was brought to us.

What are some tangible ways that others have shared the good news about Christ with you?

Sunday School, Vacation BBS, Youth group, preaching, after school Bible Study

Many people had beautiful feet in my life. Sunday school teachers, youth leaders, friends, and family members told me about Christ in a variety of ways. They taught lessons, had conversations, prayed with and for me, sent notes of encouragement, and lived lives that revealed Christ. None of them was perfect, but they gave me glimpses of Jesus.

This passage in Romans about believing, sharing, going, and sending has been widely used in missions work—and with good reason. We are all commissioned to share the good news with others.

When my husband, Sean, took a new job on staff at a church an hour away from the church we had planted where he served for ten years as senior pastor, we wanted to be careful that our church family and friends heard the news from us personally. This meant that we didn't go public about our departure until everyone in our church had the information.

In the meantime, we told our fifteen-year-old daughter that she would be transferring to a new high school. She tried out for cheerleading in our new town and was thrilled to make the varsity squad. But she couldn't tell anyone because a lot of people still didn't know we were moving. It was so hard for her not to share her good news with her friends or post about it on social media. She was bursting at the seams and so excited when she could finally tell anyone she wanted.

What good news have you shared with others lately?

Retirement

Maybe you got a great deal while shopping or your child realized a goal or got engaged. Some recent good news for me is that a medical bill wasn't as much as I had anticipated! We love to tell others when we have something to celebrate.

As I think about sharing what Jesus has done in my life, I don't always have my daughter's kind of cheerleader exuberance. I'm not sure what to say. I don't want to intrude in others' lives. I don't want to seem self-righteous or condescending. I often overcomplicate it.

Sharing the gospel can require some prayer, planning, and advice, but it doesn't have to involve a presentation, canned speech, or argument. Often it's most effective when it's natural and authentic. In talking about this recently, my pastor said that he has never seen any grandma who needed training in how to tell other people about her grandkids. It's so true, isn't it!

How have you seen a grandma tell others about her grandkids? Or how have you told others about *your* grandkids?

Grandmas often tell stories, show pictures or videos, or even reenact something cute their grandchildren have done. While I don't have any pictures of

God says we have pretty feet when we use them to take the message of His love to those who don't know Him.

Jesus on my phone, I can tell others what He has done and continues to do in my life. As we draw nearer to Jesus and appreciate more fully what He has done for us through His life, death, and resurrection, we will want to tell others how amazing He is.

I hope that studying Romans has reminded you just how good the good news actually is. We were separated from intimacy with God because of sin, and God sent His Son as a sacrifice to reconcile us. This message is worth sharing. God shows Himself in Creation but chooses to use us to communicate the message of His Son. And He says we have pretty feet when we use them to take the message of His love to those who don't know Him.

Read Matthew 28:18-20 in the margin. What were Jesus' final instructions to His followers?

To make disciples of others

¹⁸Jesus came and told his disciples, "I have been given all authority in heaven and on earth. ¹⁹Therefore, go and make disciples of all the nations, baptizing them in the name of the Father and the Son and the Holy Spirit. ²⁰Teach these new disciples to obey all the commands I have given you. And be sure of this: I am with you always, even to the end of the age."

(Matthew 28:18-20)

We are to go into all the world. Paul says in Romans 10 that at different seasons in our lives we will be go-ers and other times we will be send-ers. But we all are called to participate in enabling people to hear the gospel message so that the whole world will know there is a God who is crazy about them!

I have many friends and acquaintances who feel called to missions, moving across town or the world to commit their lives to sharing the good news about Jesus. Many of them struggle to raise the necessary prayer and financial support to carry on the work God has for them.

Take a moment to reread Romans 10:14-15, and answer these questions silently in your own heart:

- Do I really believe that Jesus' sacrifice for the sin of the world is good news for me personally?
- When was the last time I shared with another person something about the Lord?
- How am I involved in supporting missionaries through prayer and financial support?

These questions are not meant to bring us guilt but simply to challenge us to consider whether our actions reflect what we declare with our mouths and believe in our hearts. When it comes to sharing the gospel with others, a place we can start is prayer. Praying for others who are far from God softens our hearts and opens our eyes to opportunities to love them. In the same way, praying for missionaries, mission initiatives, and foreign countries by name can help us think more globally about God's mission.

If our efforts are born out of prayer, we will be less likely to turn people into projects. We don't want to nervously share memorized points. Instead, let us share our lives with others and look for opportunities to tell them about the good news that has changed everything in our lives.

Write the name of one person who is far from God and one missionary (if you don't know of a missionary, ask your church or do a search online), and take a moment to pray for them right now:

Person: *Karen*

Missionary: *Joe & Kristi*

Finally, let's remember that this good news isn't just for those who haven't heard it. We need to revisit it continually in our own lives too.

Read Romans 10:16-21. How does faith come according to verse 17?

Hearing the message through the word

In these verses Paul again provides context for the rejection of God's plan by many of the Jews. When God's plan took a right turn, many just kept going straight. They didn't move with God. They kept going their own way—to the point that they missed the Messiah. Again Paul quotes the Hebrew Scriptures several times in order to substantiate to the Jewish believers in Rome all that had happened.

Paul says the way for faith to come is through hearing—specifically, hearing the good news about Christ. Do you want your faith to grow? I know I do. This is why we stay connected in spiritual community so that we hear the good news about Christ repeatedly.

My prayer for us today is that we would appreciate those who have been the beautiful feet in our lives and that we would be beautiful feet in the lives of others!

Talk with God

Lord, I am grateful for Your message of good news. May I be beautiful feet in the lives of others, sharing Your love with them. Help me to see Your plan over the course of history so that I can make sense of what is going on in my life today. Amen.

> When it comes to sharing the gospel with others, a place we can start is prayer.

Big Idea

Faith comes by hearing God's Word.

Memory Verse Exercise

Read the Memory Verse on page 106 several times, and then fill in the blanks below as you recite it:

⁹If you _openly_ _declare_ that Jesus is _Lord_ and _believe_ in your _heart_ that God _raised_ him from the _dead_, you will be _saved_. ¹⁰For _it_ _is_ by _believing_ in your _heart_ that you are made _right_ with God, and it is by _openly_ declaring your _faith_ that you are saved.

(Romans 10:9-10)

DAY 4: THE FAMILY PLAN

Scripture Focus

Romans 11:1-24

When I sensed that my husband, Sean, might be the one I would marry, I had to have an honest conversation with him. You see, I wasn't sure I would be able to have children. I had seen a specialist at the beginning of my college years because of some problems I was having, and the doctor thought I would likely need some intervention from medication or procedures to conceive children. I felt like I needed to tell my future husband that if he married me, we might not be able to have kids. My amazing man told me he wanted to spend the rest of his life with me, and that he didn't want to marry me based on my ability to produce offspring.

Imagine our surprise when just five months into marriage we were expecting. We told everyone we would be waiting three to five years to start a family, knowing that we were young and should probably get established financially before finding out if and when we would be able to have children. Our family planning didn't turn out the way we had anticipated. After our first child was born, we grieved a miscarriage when I was seventeen weeks along and then experienced two years of infertility. When I finally became pregnant again, I had no idea I was having twins until ten days before they were born. Then we were blessed with another little girl after the twins.

I'm so grateful for the four children we were able to have, but I can tell you that our family plan was full of excitement, grief, delays, and surprises. Our situation reminds me of Proverbs 16:9, "We can make our plans, / but the LORD determines our steps."

In chapter 11 of Romans, Paul gives a very brief history of God's "family plan." God chose the nation of Israel and then grafted in the Gentiles. Unlike my experience with having kids, God knew from the beginning what His family plan would be.

○ **Read Romans 11:1-10, and write your own definition for grace based on what you've read (see vv. 5 and 6):**

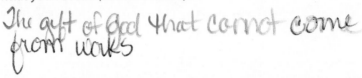
The gift of god that cannot come from works

Grace is God's kindness toward us. He gives it not based on works because it is free and undeserved. In these verses Paul once again goes to the Hebrew Scriptures to help the church understand God's plan. He isn't discounting the Israelite history of relationship with God. Right away he identifies himself as a descendant of Abraham. Then he mentions Elijah the prophet and also King David to express this truth: there has always been a remnant, a small group of people, who have truly followed God by His grace.

Jesus corroborates this statement in Matthew 7:13, saying, "You can enter God's Kingdom only through the narrow gate. The highway to hell is broad, and its gate is wide for the many who choose that way."

As we read in the Old Testament narrative, the entire nation of Israel often rebelled against God. The Lord has always distinguished between Abraham's natural children and spiritual children (John 8:38-39). In Elijah's day, a small group of faithful people worshiped Yahweh. God's plan of grace is offered to all but received only by some.

Have you ever felt in the minority as a follower of God? I can only imagine how the believers in Rome felt. The Roman culture of idolatry, slavery, and government control must have felt oppressive and discouraging. The *pax romana* or "peace of Rome" came at a great price, with the rulers bringing peace in the empire through force.

At times the fledging church must have wondered about God's plan. Why was there so much persecution and hardship? The internal squabbles between Jews and Gentiles within the house churches would have only further distracted from the mission of spreading the good news. Paul reminded the believers that God's plan is one of grace. It doesn't always make sense to our human logic, but we trust that He is kind and that we are not alone. There is always a small group of people following His way.

In your journey of faith, have you ever questioned God's plan? I've had these questions from time to time:

- Why hasn't Jesus come back yet?
- Why is life so complicated?

Extra Insight

Grafting is a gardening term. The Greek word is *egkentrizo* and means "to cut into for the sake of inserting a scion,"[9] or a shoot or bud.

Extra Insight

"The Pax Romana (Roman Peace) was a period of relative peace and stability across the Roman Empire which lasted for over 200 years, beginning with the reign of Augustus (27 BCE–14 CE)."[10]

- Why are there so many disagreements within the church?
- Why don't more people respond to the good news?

Sometimes we can be so focused on what is right in front of us that we need to zoom out for a wide-angle view. Paul gave the Roman believers a history lesson to give them perspective. God's plan started with Israel, and it has always been about grace—God's undeserved favor.

How have you experienced God's favor in your life lately?

· Things worked out for my retirement
· Prayer answered for mom, Pw's job

Some of the gals in the pilot group mentioned seeing the leaves changing in the fall (God didn't have to make it so pretty), feeling God's presence in a health journey, and enjoying friendships.

When wonderful things happen in our lives, we can acknowledge God's provision, presence, and favor. Other times God's blessings seem difficult to envision, and we may feel alone. These are moments when we must strain our eyes to look for glimpses of God's grace. Though at times we can feel outnumbered as Christians in today's culture, like Elijah we can find others who are devoted to worshiping and following Christ.

Write the names of one or two people in your life who are able to walk alongside you on your journey of faith:

Patty & Michele

God's plan may not always make sense to us, but it is always full of grace. The Greek word for grace is *charis*. I love the Strong's Concordance definition. Though it's a little long, I want you to soak in the full meaning of God's favor toward you:

> *Charis*—"good will, loving-kindness, favour; of the merciful kindness by which God, exerting his holy influence upon souls, turns them to Christ, keeps, strengthens, increases them in Christian faith, knowledge, affection, and kindles them to the exercise of the Christian virtues."[11]

The good news about God's plan is that it is good. We can trust that our God is exerting holy influence on us that is filled with merciful kindness. We will see this grace in action in this next section of Romans 11 as God grafts the Gentiles into His family tree.

Read Romans 11:11-24 and complete the labels for the illustration below. (Refer to the New Living Translation if you have trouble.)

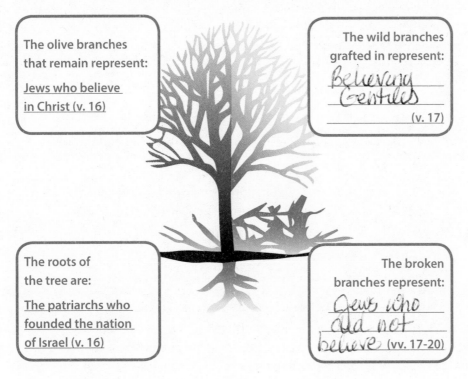

The olive branches that remain represent:

Jews who believe in Christ (v. 16)

The wild branches grafted in represent:

Believing Gentiles (v. 17)

The roots of the tree are:

The patriarchs who founded the nation of Israel (v. 16)

The broken branches represent:

Jews who did not believe (vv. 17-20)

Paul used something the people would understand. In his analogy, the roots of the tree, which are foundational, represented Abraham, Isaac, and Jacob—the patriarchs who founded the nation of Israel. The history of the Israelites is important to an understanding of God's plan. The Jews who recognized the Messiah and put their faith in Christ were the branches that remained on the olive tree. Those who did not were like dried-up branches that were pruned away so that others could be more fruitful. God then grafted the believing Gentiles into the family tree. They entered because of faith, not works.

This analogy uses something the Roman believers would have readily understood to help them see that they all are a part of God's family tree. Paul also reminds them that the Jews who choose not to accept God's grace can always come back into the tree by faith (v. 23).

What two qualities of God does Paul identify in verse 22?

Kindness & Sternness

Extra Insight

The olive tree represents the nation of Israel in the Old Testament, so Paul is drawing on a known metaphor used in Jeremiah 11:16-17 and Hosea 14:4-6.

Extra Insight

"Usually a cultivated branch is grafted into a wild tree and shares its life without producing its poor fruit. But in this case, it was the 'wild branch' (the Gentiles) that was grafted into the good tree!"[12]

Like a good parent, God is both "kind and severe," or firm—in other words, decisive in justice. He is gracious and true to His promises. He doesn't ask us to earn our way into His family tree. Instead, He invites us to believe and trust Him. By His grace He has enabled everyone to be a part of His tree. All can respond to His invitation. Yet throughout history, only a remnant of people have chosen to walk the narrow path of belief.

As we end today, take some time to think about God's plan of grace.

Where is God asking you to trust His plan in your life right now?

What to do about where to live in retirement

If you are experiencing puzzling circumstances, loneliness, or lack of direction, ask God to help you trust His plan. Write a brief prayer below:

Father God I pray for wisdom & guidance in these decisions

God's family plan includes a gracious invitation to all who will believe Him. Sean and I found that our family plan didn't turn out as we expected. Looking back, God was gracious and kind in building our family. Like a good father, the Lord keeps His promises to His people. His plan includes a remnant of believers who come together with the common goal of trusting God. Even when we feel alone, He reminds us that we are not; and He calls us to walk in faith together.

> **God's family plan includes a gracious invitation to all who will believe Him.**

Talk with God

Lord, thank You for your grace. You are kind and merciful. Help me to trust Your plan even when I don't understand it. Give me perspective as I understand the roots of our faith and see Your open invitation to all who would believe in You. Deepen my faith in your character and plan so that I might know You more. Amen.

Memory Verse Exercise

> **Big Idea**
>
> God's salvation plan includes a diverse family of all who believe and trust in Him.

Read the Memory Verse on page 106 several times, and then fill in the blanks below as you recite it:

[9]If you *openly* *declare* that *Jesus* is *Lord* and *believe* in your *heart* that *God* *raised* him *from* the *dead*, you *will* be *saved*. [10]For *it is* by *believing* in

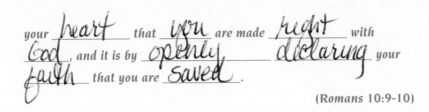

your _heart_ that _you_ are made _right_ with _God_, and it is by _openly_ _declaring_ your _faith_ that you are _saved_.

(Romans 10:9-10)

DAY 5: MYSTERIOUS PLANS

I don't like surprises. My husband has learned this the hard way after a surprise party that he lovingly planned for my thirtieth birthday didn't bring about the response he anticipated. I had to help him understand that we are wired differently. For me, half the fun of a trip or party is looking forward to it. I find joy in planning and thinking about fun things coming in the future. While my husband loves the element of mystery, I like to know what is going on.

When it comes to God's plan, He doesn't give us all the details. First Corinthians 13:9 says, "Now our knowledge is partial and incomplete, and even the gift of prophecy reveals only part of the whole picture!" So we must accept some level of ambiguity when it comes to God's plan. We can study what He has revealed in His Word, but we can't fill in the blanks God has left empty on purpose.

Read Romans 11:25-32 and answer the following questions:

What quality does Paul not want the Gentiles to display? (v. 25)

ignorance/conceit

What is the current state of some of the Israelites' hearts? (v. 25)

hardened

What hope is there for the Israelites in the future? (vv. 26-27)

they will be delivered & saved

What can never be withdrawn? (v. 29)

God's gift & his call

Our disobedience gives God an opportunity to show what to everyone? (v. 32)

mercy

Scripture Focus

Romans 11:25-36

What stood out to you as you read these verses?

God uses our weaknesses to show his strength & mercy

Maybe you read some verses that confused you. Remember that today our title is "Mysterious Plans." We may not understand everything, but we can ask, seek, and study to learn more about God and His plan.

Paul pointed out some things about both Jews and Gentiles:

- Some of the Jews have hard hearts and have missed the Messiah. Yet God will include the Jews in His future plans.
- The Gentiles have the benefit of the good news but should not be proud and should remember that God loves the people of Israel. (See John 4:22 in the Extra Insight.)

Verse 29 says that God's gifts and His call can never be withdrawn. This speaks to God's character and lines up with these Old Testament verses:

> "God is not a man, so he does not lie.
>> He is not human, so he does not change his mind.
> Has he ever spoken and failed to act?
>> Has he ever promised and not carried it through?"
>>>> (Numbers 23:19)

"I am the LORD, and I do not change."
(Malachi 3:6a)

God's character doesn't change based on people's behavior. Even though Israel was unfaithful to Him, God remained faithful to His promises.

In Romans 11:29, Paul is speaking of God's covenant promises made with Israel; but how do you think the concept that God's gifts and call can never be withdrawn applies in our lives as believers today?

We are so lost & sinful yet if we are saved & we repent we can be confident in his love & mercy

If we don't read this verse in context, we might misconstrue it to mean we can never leave a ministry or explore new callings. But one application is that God won't abandon us or take away our spiritual gifts when we return after a hard-hearted season. The Lord longs to show mercy and does not disqualify us based on past sins. Even though Israel's unbelief cut them off from God for a time, He has a plan for them. His heart is mercy and grace. If you take away anything from this week's lesson about God's plan, I pray that you will see God's

Extra Insight

"Salvation comes through the Jews."
(John 4:22)

The Lord longs to show mercy and does not disqualify us based on past sins.

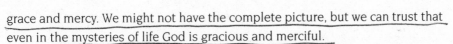

grace and mercy. We might not have the complete picture, but we can trust that even in the mysteries of life God is gracious and merciful.

I'll admit that I can't fully wrap my mind around God's plan. I have a lot of questions about why, how, when, and where. It hasn't all been revealed, so I must have faith until the time for the mysteries to be made clear. But this isn't blind faith. I'm not jumping off a random cliff into unknown waters in regard to my belief in God. My study of the Scriptures, my experiences, and my conscience lead me down a dock of sturdy theology; and when I come to the end, I then take the leap of faith. I believe that God has a plan, and His heart behind that plan is full of grace and mercy. After our leap of faith, we find ourselves worshiping the God we now trust. Warren Wiersbe says that our theology leads to doxology.[13] What I mean by this is that when we see God's amazing love and grace, our response is to praise Him.

Read Romans 11:33-36 and list some of God's qualities:

wise
knowledgable
unsearchable judgements

God is great in wisdom, riches, and knowledge. His ways are higher than ours, so we can't always understand His ways. In these verses Paul quotes the prophet Isaiah to show that God is still the same God whose thoughts are higher than ours. We cannot always know His mind, but we can trust His heart.

Summarize Romans 11:36 in your own words:

He is omnipotent, & omniscient & omni present

Everything you have comes from God. Your house, car, friends, family, job, abilities, and even your very breath are His gifts to you.

Write below something God has given you that you are thankful for right now:

Phil & Sophie

Everything exists by God's power. The sun, earth's gravity, and the oxygen level of the atmosphere make life possible for you. God sustains life and causes the sun to shine on both the wicked and the righteous (Matthew 5:45).

Write below something in creation that exists by God's power that you are grateful for today:

sun & sand

Everything is intended for God's glory. Whatever you have on your agenda today can glorify God if you do it for Him. Paul wrote these words to the church in Corinth: "So whether you eat or drink, or whatever you do, do it all for the glory of God" (1 Corinthians 10:31).

Write below how you can bring God glory today:

cooking

Even though we don't have the entire plan, we believe God does. He knows what He is doing. While I don't like surprises, I have to learn to accept that walking with God often includes some. He doesn't reveal everything. We don't understand all His ways. He is God, and we are human. We can choose to embrace His plan or fight against it. Let's take God at His Word and trust His plans more than our own.

Talk with God

Lord, I like to know the plan. Help me to trust You when I don't. Show me glimpses of Your grace and mercy when I don't understand what is going on in the world. Lord, everything I have comes from You. Everything exists by Your power, and I want to bring You glory in everything I do. Amen.

Memory Verse Exercise

Big Idea

We can't understand all of God's mysterious plans, but we can trust Him to be faithful, gracious, and merciful.

Read the Memory Verse on page 106 several times, and then fill in the blanks below as you recite it:

9 *If you openly declare that Jesus is Lord and belive in you heart that God raised him from the dead, you will be saved. For it is by believing in your heart that you are made Right with God and it is*

by _Openly_ _declaring_ your _faith_ that _you will be saved_

(Romans 10:9-10)

Weekly Wrap Up

Review the Big Idea for each day, and then write any personal application that comes to mind.

Day 1: Overlapping Truths
Big Idea: God blesses and calls His people and invites us to trust His plan.

Personal Application:_____

_____

Day 2: Relationships over Rules
Big Idea: We are not saved by the law but by declaring with our mouths and believing in our hearts the good news about Christ.

Personal Application:_____

_____

Day 3: Beautiful Feet
Big Idea: Faith comes by hearing God's Word.

Personal Application:_____

_____

Day 4: The Family Plan
Big Idea: God's salvation plan includes a diverse family of all who believe and trust in Him.

Personal Application:_____

_____

Day 5: Mysterious Plans
Big Idea: We can't understand all of God's mysterious plans, but we can trust Him to be faithful, gracious, and merciful.

Personal Application:_____

_____

VIDEO VIEWER GUIDE: WEEK 4

GOOD NEWS ABOUT GOD'S PLAN

We trust God's _____ _____ over what seems right to us.

Romans 9:19-21

Proverbs 3:5-6

Romans 9:31-32

God's plan is the _____—the good news that changes everything.

Romans 10:5-11

God's plan is too good not to _____.

Romans 10:13-17

Romans 11:33-36

Week 5

Good News About Relationships

Romans 12–14

Memory Verse

¹And so, dear brothers and sisters, I plead with you to give your bodies to God because of all he has done for you. Let them be a living and holy sacrifice—the kind he will find acceptable. This is truly the way to worship him. ²Don't copy the behavior and customs of this world, but let God transform you into a new person by changing the way you think. Then you will learn to know God's will for you, which is good and pleasing and perfect.

(Romans 12:1-2)

DAY 1: LASTING CHANGE

My sweet friend Tanya has told me many stories regarding her past, referring to herself as "Old Tanya." Before she was a Christian, Tanya was an executive who would admit she didn't treat people well. I told her that, knowing her now as a kind and loving person who seeks Jesus with her whole heart, I don't believe in "Old Tanya." How could she have been so dramatically different? She assured me that "Old Tanya" was real.

Then one day Tanya had car trouble. I told her I had the name of a wonderful Christian mechanic. When I gave her the name and number, she took a gulp and mentioned that decades earlier this man had worked at the same company as she did. She said she would need to apologize for the behavior of "Old Tanya" before asking him to help with her vehicle. Later my husband spoke with our mechanic and friend, who said that he had heard from Tanya and was amazed she is now a follower of Christ. He could hardly believe it. He kept repeating these words, "Wow, that is incredible." I guess Tanya wasn't exaggerating.

Life change might not be as noticeable for you as it was for Tanya, but all of us who follow Christ have been transformed. The "Old Melissa" was without hope before the good news about Christ changed everything in my life.

Can you identify one aspect of your life that has changed since you began following Christ? If so, write about it below:

Some changes we all share are hope for this life and the life to come, greater clarity in our purpose as we seek to share God's message of love with others, and character that is in the process of being conformed to the image of Christ.

The change in Tanya's life was noticeable, and the same was true of the apostle Paul, also called Saul (see Acts 13:9). He certainly had some stories about "Old Paul"—a Pharisee, a strict rule-follower, and a persecutor of followers of Christ who wanted them to be stopped at any cost. Then something changed everything. Jesus spoke to Saul in a blinding light on the road as he was traveling to Damascus to persecute Christians. The Lord asked why Saul was persecuting Him and told him to go into the city and wait for instructions. This encounter caused Paul to undergo a spiritual metamorphosis.

Twenty-five years after this experience on the road, Paul urged the Roman church to live changed lives, writing some of the most quoted verses in all of Scripture.

Scripture Focus

Romans 12:1-2

Digging Deeper

In speaking of offering ourselves as living sacrifices, Romans 12:1-2 references the sacrificial system of animal offerings. What connections can we make between the Hebrew systems of animal sacrifice, Christ's ultimate sacrifice, and our call to offer our lives as holy sacrifices? Check out the Digging Deeper article for Week 5, "Come to the Altar" (see AbingdonWomen .com/Romans).

Extra Insight

You can read Paul's story of transformation in Acts 9.

Read Romans 12:1-2 and write Paul's instructions to believers in your own words below:

To offer yourself, mind and body, to God, living in a way that honors him

These verses don't contain suggestions. Paul was pleading with the church. He used the Greek word *parakaleo*, whose meaning lies between commanding and beseeching.[1] This wasn't a recommendation but an imperative statement calling them to:

- Give their bodies to God as living and holy sacrifices
- Not conform to this world
- Be transformed by the renewing of their minds

When Paul followed the Jewish law, he would have looked to animal sacrifices to atone for his sin. Now as a follower of Christ, he understands that Christ died as the final sacrifice for sin. As Hebrews 10:10 says, "For God's will was for us to be made holy by the sacrifice of the body of Jesus Christ, once for all time." So we must understand that in verse 1, Paul is not talking about sacrifice in terms of payment for sin. Instead, he is talking about worship in regard to our sanctification where we are becoming more like Christ in our daily walk.

In this vein, Paul says that we can worship God by dying to ourselves. We put our bodies on the altar and yield to His ways over our own. Some everyday examples of this might be praying when our flesh wants to watch television, forgiving when we want to take revenge, or giving to others when we feel like buying more stuff for ourselves. Worship isn't just a Sunday morning event; it is the continual process of choosing to follow God's instructions rather than what seems right or feels good in the moment. This requires sacrifice.

Paul goes on in verse 2 to use two verbs to explain this process more fully. Take a moment to read this verse in the Amplified Bible (Classic Edition) (AMPC):

> Do not be conformed to this world (this age), [fashioned after and adapted to its external, superficial customs], but be transformed (changed) by the [entire] renewal of your mind [by its new ideals and its new attitude], so that you may prove [for yourselves] what is the good and acceptable and perfect will of God, even *the thing which is good and acceptable and perfect* [in His sight for you].

First Paul tells us what not to do. We are not to copy or conform to the patterns and behavior of this world. He uses the verb *suschematizo*, which means

"to conform one's self (i.e., one's mind and character) to another's pattern, (fashion one's self according to)."[2]

Then he uses a passive verb to tell us what we should do. *Metamorphoo* means "to change into another form, to transform, to transfigure."[3] Perhaps this word reminds you of an English word.

What images come to mind when you hear the word *metamorphosis*?

Taking a whole new form
Caterpillar → butterfly

I thought of tadpoles transforming into frogs or caterpillars changing into butterflies. God wants to change us, but it doesn't happen by us trying harder. The Greek verb *metamorphoo* is passive because it is something God does as we yield to Him. Our part in this change comes by allowing the Lord to change the way we think.

The apostle Paul's life took a 180-degree turn when he began to follow Christ. Instead of persecuting Christians, he began telling everyone he could about Jesus. Yet even for Paul, there also was an ongoing process of spiritual growth. As believers, the practice of renewing our minds is an ongoing process, not a one-time thing, which leads to growth. We constantly have to be on guard not to be conformed to the patterns and behaviors of this world.

In your opinion, what are some of the worldly patterns and behaviors that we must not conform to? (There are many answers; just pick two or three.)

Being angry & impacient
Putting ourselves first
Being greedy & covetting

You might have thought of selfishness, greed, lust, jealousy, pride, or something else. We could talk about the evils of the world all day long, but we want to focus on change. And as Paul said, when it comes to allowing God to transform us, it begins with the renewing of our minds.

What are some practical ways that you renew your mind to allow Christ to bring change (metamorphosis) in your life?

Reading the Bible
Praying
Worship w/ believers

I asked this question on social media and received a variety of responses. As you read through the list below, put a star beside any

Extra Insight

The Greek word for transformed, *metamorphoo*, is the same word used in Mark 9:2 for Christ being transfigured on a mountain where his appearance became dazzling white in front of Peter, James, and John.

When it comes to allowing God to transform us, it begins with the renewing of our minds.

that you already practice regularly. Put a checkmark next to any that you would like to incorporate into your life:

_____ Sitting quietly and intentionally focusing on Jesus

_____ Using discernment to think biblically about information I receive from television/movies and social media

___✓___ Identifying irrational or ungodly thoughts and taking them "captive" (2 Corinthians 10:5) to gain control over what I am thinking about

___✗___ Reading, interpreting, and applying God's Word

_____ Listening to worship music

_____ Journaling

___✓___ Memorizing Scripture

_____ Running alone on a road or path without any technology

___✗___ Staying engaged with other believers

___✗___ Praying (including praying God's Word)

___✗___ Thanking God specifically for what He has done (making a gratitude list)

___✗___ Being in nature and admiring God's handiwork

_____ Being intentional to talk and listen to God while I drive or walk

___✗___ Exercising

_____ Listening to podcasts or sermons

___✗___ Spending time with godly friends or mentors

Our brain has two sides. Our left hemisphere is the center of our logic and reason, and we renew our minds using this side of our brains by talking to God and reading, studying, and memorizing His Word. Imagination and creativity take place in the right hemisphere of our brains. Activities such as silence, listening prayer, worship music, dance, and journaling can realign this portion of our minds.

Dr. Caroline Leaf has done research on the neurological aspects of mind renewal. Her excellent book *Switch On Your Brain* has technical information and

practical tips related to mind renewal. She writes, "You cannot sit back and wait to be happy and healthy and have a great thought life; you have to make the choice to make this happen. You have to choose to get rid of the toxic and get back in alignment with God. You can be overwhelmed by every small setback in life, or you can be energized by the possibilities they bring."[4] While God does the transformation within us, we can choose either to let our thoughts run wild or to surrender them to God.

So much of our spiritual battle takes place in our thought lives. We have many options vying to feed our minds with information. Social media, television, radio, podcasts, books, and daydreams can shape our thinking toward God or away from Him. We must be careful with what we allow in and out of our thoughts. We need the Holy Spirit to help us take thoughts captive and guide us toward redemptive thinking.

> **After reflecting on Romans 12:1-2, what type of changes would you like to implement when it comes to your thought life?**
>
> *Taking in more "godly" information during the week*

For myself, I would like to think more positive and hopeful thoughts. In a world full of bad news, this requires intentionality. Dr. Leaf tells us, "Thoughts are real, physical things that occupy mental real estate. Moment by moment, every day, you are changing the structure of your brain through your thinking. When we hope, it is an activity of the mind that changes the structure of our brain in a positive and normal direction."[5] My prayer is that studying Romans will do just that—literally change the structure of our brains in a more positive and hopeful direction. And here is some good news to claim as we end today: As we renew our minds, we will learn to know God's good and pleasing and perfect will in our lives!

Talk with God

Lord, I want to love You with all of my heart, soul, mind, and strength. Help me to guard and evaluate what I think about. Show me how to renew my mind with Your truth. Reveal anything I need to stop allowing into my thoughts. I want to learn to take thoughts captive and allow You to transform me from the inside out! Amen.

Memory Verse Exercise

> **Read the Memory Verse on page 136 several times, and then fill in the blanks on the following page as you recite it:**

Big Idea

We continually offer ourselves as living sacrifices and allow God to change us through the renewing of our minds.

[1]And so, dear brothers and sisters, I _plead_ with you to give your _bodies_ to God because of all he has done for you. Let them be a _living_ and _holy_ sacrifice—the kind he will find acceptable. This is truly the way to _worship_ him. [2]Don't copy the _behaviors_ and customs of this world, but let God transform you into a new person by changing the way you _think_. Then you will learn to know God's will for you, which is good and pleasing and perfect.

(Romans 12:1-2)

DAY 2: BULLFROGS AND BUTTERFLIES

Scripture Focus

Romans 12:3-21

Recently I had the opportunity to visit a women's Bible study group and share about my personal journey of faith. Afterward, the leader asked if anyone had questions for me. One woman asked about the Bible college I attended and another about how I choose the topics for my Bible studies. Then one woman said she had a question but wasn't sure if it was too personal.

I had mentioned something about growing up with a family member who struggled with anger and then later about this same person doing missions work. She asked if there had been a transformation in this person's life regarding anger. Out of nowhere I found myself emotional. It's a tender topic for me. Several people close to me have struggled with anger. I've seen them grow in their ability to overcome anger as they have struggled with it for decades. Here's the deal: we all have our own sin tendencies. Our struggle might not be with anger but with selfishness, pride, laziness, complaining, or some other sin.

In what area of your life would you like to see transformation right now? _complaining_

How would change in this area impact your closest relationships?

It really wouldn't but it would help @ work

Perhaps you are working on becoming more thoughtful, kind, or content or are developing some other godly quality. Maybe you are healing from an addiction or are in the process of kicking a sinful habit. We all have room to grow in the process of sanctification.

After Paul urged the believers in Rome to put their lives on the altar as living sacrifices and encouraged them to renew their minds, he then gave examples of the changes that are produced by Christ through this process. Tadpoles turn into bullfrogs and caterpillars transform into butterflies. As believers, we become more and more like Christ, and our changes affect not only our personal attitudes and behaviors but also our relationships.

Read Romans 12:3-8 and list what a changed person's life might reveal according to the prompts below:

A ___*sober*___ evaluation of themselves (v. 3)

The ability to see themselves as part of Christ's ___*body*___ (vv. 4-5)

___*made*___ **for serving others (vv. 6-8)**

As I reflect on each of these qualities, I notice that they are not the patterns and behaviors of selfishness and independence. Instead they reveal an others-centered posture of interdependence. Through the renewing of our minds, Christ transforms us to see our need for Him and others. True change happens as we begin to see ourselves as valued by God and commissioned by Him to use our gifts in significant ways.

Scripture tells us that the Holy Spirit is the source of all spiritual gifts and gives one to every believer (1 Corinthians 12:4, 7). Have you identified your spiritual gift?

What is one spiritual gift you either know or suspect you have, and how are you using it to benefit others within the body of Christ?

Contributing to the needs of others

If you aren't sure what gift you have, a good starting place would be talking with a mentor, Bible study leader, or friend. An online questionnaire also can be a helpful tool for discovering your spiritual gifts (see Extra Insight in the margin). Using our gifts serves others but also brings spiritual energy into our lives.

I have been involved in middle school ministry for many years. Often when I have taught a middle school Bible study, I have left physically and even

Extra Insight

A number of ancient writers used "the body" as a metaphor for a political state. "A few writers even called the state the 'body' of the emperor."[6]

Extra Insight

For more detailed descriptions of the gifts and to take a survey, see www. ministrymatters.com /spiritualgifts (set up a free account and then take the survey), www .spiritualgiftstest.com /test/adult, or another online spiritual gifts inventory. (You might find it helpful to take more than one survey and compare the results.)

Extra Insight

The list of gifts in Romans 12 is not complete. First Corinthians 12, Ephesians 4, and 1 Peter 4 reveal more gifts and details for study.

emotionally tired but spiritually revitalized. We were created to serve others in the unique ways God has gifted us, and allowing Him to work through us benefits us as well.

How have you experienced spiritual renewal and personal growth as you've used your gifts to serve others?

It's envigorating to pack the Christmas boxes

I used to do nursery, Sunday school, youth group

As you've encouraged, given generously, showed kindness, taught, or led others, I wonder if you've met people, experienced joy, or seen God work in ways that strengthened your faith. Becoming a living sacrifice doesn't end with humility and using our gifts to serve each other. The transformation Christ works within us affects our relationships in many significant ways.

Paul goes on in Romans 12:9-21 to laundry-list some commands that also are markers of a redeemed life, which I've listed below.

Put a checkmark beside the markers that *directly* mention relationships with others:

✓ 1. "Don't just pretend to love others. Really love them." (v. 9)

____ 2. "Hate what is wrong." (v. 9)

____ 3. "Hold tightly to what is good." (v. 9)

✓ 4. "Love each other with genuine affection . . ." (v. 10)

✓ 5. ". . . and take delight in honoring each other." (v. 10)

____ 6. "Never be lazy, but work hard and serve the Lord enthusiastically." (v. 11)

____ 7. "Rejoice in our confident hope." (v. 12)

____ 8. "Be patient in trouble . . ." (v. 12)

____ 9. ". . . and keep on praying." (v. 12)

✓ 10. "When God's people are in need, be ready to help them." (v. 13)

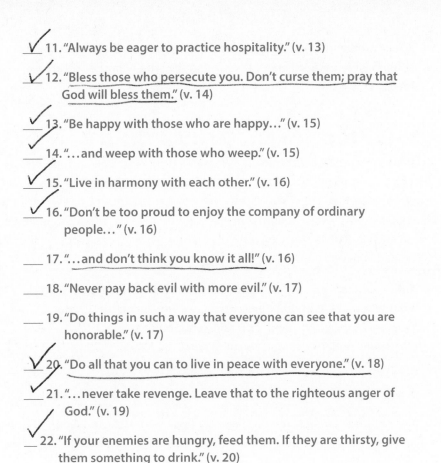

✓ 11. "Always be eager to practice hospitality." (v. 13)

✓ 12. "Bless those who persecute you. Don't curse them; pray that God will bless them." (v. 14)

✓ 13. "Be happy with those who are happy…" (v. 15)

✓ 14. "…and weep with those who weep." (v. 15)

✓ 15. "Live in harmony with each other." (v. 16)

✓ 16. "Don't be too proud to enjoy the company of ordinary people…" (v. 16)

____ 17. "…and don't think you know it all!" (v. 16)

____ 18. "Never pay back evil with more evil." (v. 17)

____ 19. "Do things in such a way that everyone can see that you are honorable." (v. 17)

✓ 20. "Do all that you can to live in peace with everyone." (v. 18)

____ 21. "…never take revenge. Leave that to the righteous anger of God." (v. 19)

✓ 22. "If your enemies are hungry, feed them. If they are thirsty, give them something to drink." (v. 20)

____ 23. "Don't let evil conquer you, but conquer evil by doing good." (v. 21)

Extra Insight

Paul wrote Romans 12:9-21 using an ancient style called *paraenesis*. It included moral exhortation, it borrowed from many sources, and it was loosely structured. This style was well known in the ancient world and therefore familiar to his readers.[7]

While many of these commands directly mention relationships, all of them ultimately impact the way we relate with others.

As you read these commands taken from Romans 12:9-21 (NLT), which ones stood out most to you? Go back and underline two or three statements that really hit home where you are right now.

The one that really gets me is the very first one. Your translation may say that love must be sincere or without hypocrisy. I love the wording of the New Living Translation: "Don't pretend to love others. Really love them." The Greek word used for "don't pretend" is *anypokritos*, which is literally "not hypocritical" and is "often applied to the actor who 'played a part' on the stage."[8] When it comes to loving, we shouldn't fake it. People should not become our projects. We don't treat them well to make ourselves look righteous or to manipulate situations. God says that when He transforms us by the renewing of our minds, we will really love others the way He does.

Answers: 1, 4, 5, 10, 11, 12, 13, 14, 15, 16, 19, 20, 22

Take a moment to read Romans 12:9-21 in your own Bible. What shift do you notice in verse 14 regarding the type of people we are interacting with?

They are not necessarily fellow believers / different from us

Paul starts with encouraging the Roman believers to love each other well. Then he begins talking about those who persecute us or do things that would tempt us to take revenge. We have to remember that these churches were a religious minority facing potential persecution from soldiers, family members, and neighbors. Paul is renewing Jesus' call to non-retaliation as a way of life for persecuted believers (see Matthew 5:44; Luke 6:27-28).

Take a moment and think about your most strained relationship right now. Whether it is another believer or someone persecuting you because of your faith, who is pressing your buttons lately?
(Write one initial if you don't want to write the name.)

hT

We can't genuinely love and forgive on our own. We need God's help to transform us by the renewing of our minds. This means we have to die to our own desires for revenge. We have to admit that we don't know it all.

Take some time to prayerfully reflect on the truths we've read today by following the prompts below.

- Pray for those you are struggling to treat in the way that Romans 12:9-21 instructs.
- As you look over this list, evaluate where God has changed you and where you still have room to grow.
- Ask God to heal any fractured relationships and help you see others the way He does.

Record some thoughts from your reflection and prayer time:

Though we are in the process of being transformed, our ultimate metamorphosis will come in eternity. For now, sin still impacts our lives

because we live in a fallen world. This affects our relationships. We all need the good news that changes everything. As we live in overlapping ages of already and not yet, our transformation is not yet complete and does not always show externally. Sanctification is a process, but we live by faith that Christ's death and life will redeem not only our eternities but also our relationships in the here and now!

Talk with God

Lord, I thank You for these truths in Romans, acknowledging that You embody all of the qualities we read about today. You don't pretend to love us; You really do. You never pay back evil with evil. You forgive. You conquered evil by doing good, sending Jesus to die in my place. Thank You, Lord. Help me to allow You to transform me into a person like the one these verses describe. Amen.

Memory Verse Exercise

Read the Memory Verse on page 136 several times, and then fill in the blanks below as you recite it:

¹And so, dear __brothers__ and sisters, I __pleade__ with you to give your __bodies__ to God __because__ of all he has done for you. Let them be a __living__ and __holy__ sacrifice—the kind he will find __acceptable__. This is truly the way to __worship__ him. ²Don't copy the __behavior__ and customs of this __world__, but let God transform you into a new person by __changing__ the way you __think__. Then you will learn to know God's will for you, which is good and __pleasing__ and perfect.

(Romans 12:1-2)

Big Idea

When we allow Christ to transform us by the renewing of our minds, it affects our relationships in incredible ways.

DAY 3: LOVE AND RESPECT

This year I've enjoyed watching some television shows about kings and queens. I'm fascinated by the respect, decorum, and rules during historical monarchies through the centuries. Having grown up in a country that values independence, checks and balances, and representative leaders, I found myself intrigued by the amount of leadership responsibility a monarchy places on one human being. Just as a monarchy is much different than a democracy, so also the Roman government at the time of Paul's writing looked much different than

Scripture Focus

Romans 13:1-10

anything we have experienced. The authorities referenced by Paul in the passage from Romans 13 that we will study today could have included the emperor, senate, consuls, and magistrates, as well as the military forces associated with them.[9] Roman government brought order to areas on the verge of anarchy. The problem in many areas of the Roman Empire wasn't too much government but too little. The Roman government brought public order, punishment for criminals, and a sense of common good, yet it also committed atrocities and enforced peace with a sword.

As we open Romans 13 today, we will find biblical instruction for showing respect for authority and love for one another. We must understand the backdrop of the Roman context in order to see Paul's heart behind his teaching. The passage begins by addressing our relationship with governing authorities.

Read Romans 13:1-7 and answer the following questions:

To whom are we to submit? (vv. 1, 5)

governing authorities

Who placed people in positions of governmental authority? (vv. 1, 4)

God

Why did God give authorities? (v. 4)

To do good & punish wrongdoers

Why should we submit to authorities? (v. 5)

punishment & conscience

Why should we pay taxes? (v. 6)

Because we owe them

What should we give to those in authority? (v. 7)

What you owe: taxes, revenue, respect

What is your initial reaction to these verses?

It is very hard in 2019

Do you think there are any exceptions to these instructions? If so, what are they?

If they become corrupt & work against God

Many students of Paul's Letter to the Romans have been unsettled by these instructions. The early church father Origen, who knew about Roman brutality firsthand, said, "I am disturbed by Paul's saying that the authority of this age and the judgment of the world are ministers of God."[10] We might have similar feelings as we think about our government leaders, so we must consider Paul's purposes related to the original audience of his letter. With anti-Roman zeal on the rise during Paul's ministry, perhaps he wanted the church to be certain that he would be coming to Rome in the future as a missionary, not a political activist. He wanted the church to keep their focus on the good news that changes everything rather than joining a revolutionary political movement. He wanted believers to pray and respect their leaders while putting their energy into sharing the gospel message.

We must exercise good interpretation by looking at the whole of Scripture and asking whether instances of civil disobedience are ever endorsed. After Peter and the apostles were instructed by the ruling authorities not to teach in Jesus' name, they responded by saying, "We must obey God rather than any human authority" (Acts 5:29). Likewise, the Letter to the Hebrews references the story of Moses' parents hiding him by faith: "They saw that God had given them an unusual child, and they were not afraid to disobey the king's command" (Hebrews 11:23). Based on these two examples, we see that unqualified obedience to the state is not Paul's intent in Romans 13.

Can you think of some historical or modern-day examples of times when submitting to the government might not be the best option?

Germany during Hitler

Dietrich Bonhoeffer was a German pastor who lived under the Nazi regime and grappled with the idea of submitting to a totalitarian government that committed atrocities. After seeking wisdom from God and others, he ultimately believed that standing silent in the face of evil was ethically unacceptable. He participated in a failed attempt to assassinate Hitler and was imprisoned and executed in a concentration camp. Stories like his and many others illustrate that Paul's teaching gives general guidelines rather than strict moral absolutes when it comes to our relationship with governing authorities. These instructions had an original audience with unique circumstances. We need the Holy Spirit to help us live and act in a way that best represents Christ as we seek to live out these verses.

I love how commentator Michael Bird summarizes practical applications from this text:

Wherever a menacing empire casts its shadow—whether from the east or from the west—Christians have a responsibility to order their lives around the story and symbols of Jesus. We are to live our lives as exemplary citizens, and we must yet let it be known that our loyalty is owed first and foremost to the true Lord of the world.[11]

As we take Paul's words to heart and seek to honor our leaders, we also realize that when human authority asks us to live counter to divine authority, we must go with God!

What are some practical ways that, as believers, we can honor our governing authorities?

As I studied this passage, I recalled a concept that was taught to me in my young adult years:

We honor the position of authority even when the person holding it isn't worthy of respect.

Whether it is parents, teachers, coaches, police officers, or government leaders, we can speak respectfully and honor the positions they hold. This does not mean we agree with everything they say or do.

As you consider the way you think, speak, or act toward those in authority, how might God be calling you to a more respectful tone? Write anything that comes to mind below:

Frustration w/ Pete

Extra Insight

At the time of Paul's writing, the Roman emperor Nero was fairly well behaved in the early years of his reign. Later Nero became violent toward Christians and was the ruler who sentenced Paul to death.[12]

These first verses in Romans 13 have caused me to pause and think. Social media is a place where I see respect greatly lacking. What is called "keyboard courage" can lead us to engage without face-to-face tact. Let's allow Paul's teaching on respect to sink in and ask God to show us how we can best represent Him in all our relationships—even when it comes to those in authority over us who may or may not be worthy of our respect.

Next Paul moves from showing respect to showing love. Having talked about paying taxes and giving to everyone what you owe them, Paul now says there is one good debt to have.

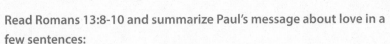

Read Romans 13:8-10 and summarize Paul's message about love in a few sentences:

Loving others is the supreme law and if you do it all of the other commands will follow

This section begins with an admonition to owe nothing to anyone but love. The metaphor of debt is one we can relate to today. In a world full of credit cards and advertisements to buy now and pay later, we understand the concept of being overextended. One commentator framed it this way: "Imagine that love is a credit card with no borrowing limit, and your job is try to max it out. Make yourself indebted and obligated to love others. Make your love higher than the interest rates on an American Express card. The best way to avoid moral bankruptcy is to rack up love-based debts."[13]

When love abounds, the law is fulfilled. Love meets God's requirements. The way we love others may look very different for each of us. Sometimes love speaks painful truth and other times it covers a multitude of sins. First Corinthians 13:4-7 gives us this description of what love can look like:

> [4]Love is patient and kind. Love is not jealous or boastful or proud [5]or rude. It does not demand its own way. It is not irritable, and it keeps no record of being wronged. [6]It does not rejoice about injustice but rejoices whenever the truth wins out. [7]Love never gives up, never loses faith, is always hopeful, and endures through every circumstance.

I wonder how the Lord is calling you to love right now. What is one way you can max out your love credit card today?

Continue to pray for my colleagues & friends rather than get frustrated w/ them

Today the Lord is calling me to be patient with myself and others. I always want to read more, write more, listen more, do more, and be more. I forget to savor and celebrate what God is doing when I strive toward productivity. In my quest for more I can be tempted to miss opportunities to love right where I am. So today I hear God's voice to slow down and love. I pray that you are hearing His loving voice in your life as well. As you listen and respond, you will see first-hand that love and respect are good news for our relationships.

> Sometimes love speaks painful truth and other times it covers a multitude of sins.

Talk with God

Lord, help me to understand what it means to honor the governing authorities in my life. Let my ultimate allegiance be to You, Jesus. Show me what it means to respect and love others. I want to max out my love credit card by allowing You to love others through me. Give me eyes to see opportunities to love today. Amen.

Memory Verse Exercise

Read the Memory Verse on page 136 several times, and then fill in the blanks below as you recite it:

¹*And so, dear* __brothers__ *and sisters, I* __plead__ *with you to give your* __bodies__ *to God* __because__ *of all he has done for you. Let them be a* __living__ *and* __holy__ *sacrifice—the* __kind__ *he will find* __acceptable__*. This is truly the way to* __worship__ *him.* ²*Don't* __let copy__ *the* __behaviors__ *and customs of this* __world__*, but let God* __transform__ *you into a new person by* __changing__ *the way you* __think__*. Then you will learn to know* __God's__ __will__ *for you, which is good and* __pleasing__ *and* __perfect__*.*

(Romans 12:1-2)

DAY 4: BELIEF AND BEHAVIOR

Scripture Focus

Romans 13:11-14

Many years ago I was coerced into participating in a mud run with a group of friends. Mud and running are two things at the bottom of my list of favorites. Someone paid for my entry, and my husband said he would feel loved and valued if I completed the race with him. So I did it. Soon after we began running, the course required sliding down a muddy hill into a pile of mud. At another point we swam under barbed wire in pools of dirty water. My shoes and clothes became heavy with mud, which made running and even walking difficult. All this to say I'm glad my husband enjoyed the adventure, but you will find me at a similar event in the future only if it's on the sidelines.

That mud was a lot like sinful deeds. Just as the mud slowed down all the participants in the mud run, so our sin weighs us down in the race of life. Today we will find Paul instructing us to take off our sinful deeds so that we can pursue Jesus uninhibited.

Big Idea

God calls us to honor our governing authorities and to love others.

Read Romans 13:11-14 and draw or describe what we are to take off and put on according to verse 12:

We need to take off all of our ugly, dirty deeds and focus on God alone

We put off deeds of darkness and put on God's armor of light. The New Living Translation says it this way, "The night is almost gone; the day of salvation will soon be here. So remove your dark deeds like dirty clothes, and put on the shining armor of right living" (v. 12). These verses instruct us to

- Live in the light of Jesus' return
- Take off our sinful deeds like dirty clothes
- Clothe ourselves with the presence of Jesus

Before we dive into these topics, I wonder if you might be thinking something like this: "So far we've been learning that the good news is all about faith and not the law. So why does this feel like the focus has shifted to rules? I thought belief in Christ was the good news, but now the instructions seem to be more about behaving well."

What thoughts or questions do you have about the roles of belief and behavior in regard to salvation?

Even though our salvation is not dependent on our deeds, our behavior is what can show God to the world

As I've asked my own questions about this, I've found that understanding what comes first is extremely important. If we start with behavior and try to do everything right, we find ourselves in the legalism trap that we've discussed previously. The Pharisees fell into the behavior camp. When we begin with faith and place our trust in Christ, then God's Spirit takes up residence inside us, resulting in our love for God overflowing into love for others.

These instructions in Romans 13:11-14 come on the heels of Paul's message about love fulfilling the law (verses 8-10). So he isn't saying, "Be really good so God will love you." Phil Yancey says it well: "Grace means there is nothing I can do to make God love me more, and nothing I can do to make God love me less. It means that I, even I who deserve the opposite, am invited to take my place at the table in God's family."[14]

If salvation is all about grace and faith, then why is Paul telling the Roman believers how to behave—to wake up, put off dark deeds, and clothe themselves with Christ? Why does it matter what we do if only faith can save us?

To answer this, let's recall our lesson in Week 3 on the difference between justification, sanctification, and glorification (see page 77). Here in Romans 13:11-14, Paul isn't referencing justification—the aspect of salvation when God declares us righteous through our faith in Christ. Rather, Paul is teaching about our sanctification—the continual process of being conformed to the image of Christ. When it comes to our behavior, God longs for us to make right choices because He loves us.

As you consider the rules, discipline, and instruction that parents give to their children, why do you think most parents want their children to behave well? *They want what is best for them and they want them to grow up to make good choices*

I don't love my kids more when they choose wisely, but I want them to behave well for their own good. I know that living according to God's instructions leads to life, helping us to avoid the suffering brought on by sin. The reason I teach, correct, and advise my children springs from my love for them. My parenting is far from perfect, but my motive is so that they won't run through life with the muck of sin weighing them down.

How would you sum up the relationship between belief and behavior in regard to salvation? (Don't overthink it; just write a sentence or two.) *We are saved bc of our belief but we always have to work @ the behavior that shows it*

When the New Testament teaches about behavior or right living, the instructions are not about earning grace but about living love. Our behavior springs from our belief that God is good and His ways are worth following.

Reread Romans 13:11. What is Paul's instruction to believers? *Love people now*

Our behavior springs from our belief that God is good and His ways are worth following.

After telling us about the priority of love, Paul tells us that love should wake us up. Like the believers living in Rome, we can slumber in apathy, boredom, or distraction so easily in our culture. Paul reminds us that love should compel us to remember that Jesus is coming back. So many people need to hear about this good news that changes everything. <u>As D. L. Moody said, "Out of 100 [people],</u> <u>one will read the Bible, the other 99 will read the Christian."[15]</u> Paul is essentially saying that our mission is urgent—like waking up in a burning building and telling others to get out. No one apathetically warns their family about a fire. Paul urges us to flee from things that will get us off course from our love and purpose in Christ.

Have you struggled with any apathy, boredom, or distraction in your faith lately? If so, describe it briefly:

I feel like I'm always distracted by obligations

What are some things that wake you up to the priority of faith and action? *Seeing others suffer, or suffering myself makes me realize the importance of my faith*

Reading Romans continues to be a good wake-up call for me. I pray it is for you as well. We must fight our human tendency to forget about God and His good news. As we think about Christ's return, it motivates us to live in the light of His coming. I love the illustration Paul uses of stripping off our dark deeds and clothing ourselves with God's armor of light.

After I finished the mud run, all I wanted to do was change into clean clothes and shoes. However, the event took place in a field with only portable bathrooms and a lake. I should say it was more of a filthy pond full of other participants trying to get clean. Sometimes we try to do this spiritually. We try to clean ourselves up from bad habits, temptations, and fleshly desires, but we can't manage our sin. We need Christ to wash us through the power of His blood shed on the cross and then clothe us with His armor of right living.

What does Romans 13:14 say we should clothe ourselves with?

the Lord

Christ is our armor of light. It is Christ's presence that enables us to make godly choices.

In Ephesians 6:10-17 we find a list of spiritual armor that we can wear to help us fight spiritual battles. Each piece of armor is Jesus Himself. He is truth (belt), our righteousness (breastplate), our peace (shoes), the author and perfecter of our faith (shield), our salvation (helmet), and the living Word (sword). When we

Extra Insight

In other writings of Paul, he seems to imply that Christ will not return until after he (Paul) is gone (2 Corinthians 5:1-10; Philippians 1:20-24). One commentator writes, "His belief about the proximity of Christ's return was not imminent, but more like an intense notion of nearness."[16]

invite Jesus close—from the top of our heads to the bottom of our feet, He helps us win our battles.

Paul knew the Roman Christians were fighting against the flesh or sinful nature and the immoral culture. He was well aware of the drinking parties and religious festivals in Roman culture when he referenced the drunkenness, wild parties, fighting, and sexual promiscuity of the darkness. One commentator says, "Greco-Roman revelry could make a frat house toga party look like a convent in comparison."[17] The believers in Rome needed to stay on guard against the lure of things surrounding them. We too must consider the party culture in which we live.

Even in Christian circles, sexual immorality and drunkenness can become normalized. Instead of judging others or raging on social media, we must look at our own hearts and ask how we can throw off our own darkness and embrace Christ's presence as armor. As we consider what we "consume" in our culture, we can ask this question: Is *it darkness*?

God is calling us into the light—not to earn His love but to grow in it. Let's close today by reading some verses about light.

> **God is calling us into the light—not to earn His love but to grow in it.**

Read the verses below, and circle any words or phrases that stand out to you:

Your word is a lamp to guide my feet
and a light for my path.
(Psalm 119:105)

[34]*"Your eye is like a lamp that provides light for your body. When your eye is healthy, your whole body is filled with light. But when it is unhealthy, your body is filled with darkness.* [35]*Make sure that the light you think you have is not actually darkness."*

(Luke 11:34-35)

Jesus spoke to the people once more and said, "I am the light of the world. If you follow me, you won't have to walk in darkness, because you will have the light that leads to life."

(John 8:12)

[5]*This is the message we heard from Jesus and now declare to you: God is light, and there is no darkness in him at all.* [6]*So we are lying if we say we have fellowship with God but go on living in spiritual darkness; we are not practicing the truth.* [7]*But if we are living in the light, as God is in the light, then we have fellowship with each other, and the blood of Jesus, his Son, cleanses us from all sin.*

(1 John 1:5-7)

What are the truths related to these words or phrases that resonate with you? *There is no darkness in Christ He is our only way out of darkness*

The one that jumped off the page for me was, "Make sure that the light you think you have is not actually darkness" (Luke 11:35). The related truth is that I must ask God to grant me discernment to see things clearly.

Review again the main lessons of today's passage, and circle the one that challenges you most:

Live in the light of Jesus' return.

Take off our sinful deeds like dirty clothes.

Clothe ourselves with the presence of Jesus.

These behaviors impact our relationships with God and others. God longs for us to make these right choices not because they save us but because they conform us to the image of Christ. Remember, our God is good, and His ways are worth following because they are good—not only for us but also for our relationships.

Talk with God

Lord, give me a right understanding of belief and behavior. I want to throw off my dark deeds like dirty clothes. Come and clothe me in Your presence with the armor of right living. Reveal areas that need change, and empower me to do it! Amen.

Memory Verse Exercise

Read the Memory Verse on page 136 several times, and then fill in the blanks below as you recite it:

¹And so, dear **brothers** and sisters, I **plead** with you to **offer** your **bodies** to God **because** of all he has **done** for you. Let them be a **living** and **holy** sacrifice—the **kind** he will find **acceptable**. This is **truly** the way to **worship** him. ²Don't **copy** the **beliefs** and customs of this **world**, but **let** God **transform**

Big Idea

Our belief in Jesus overflows into right behavior.

you into a new *person* by *Changing* the way you *think*. Then you will *learn* to know *Gods will* for you, which is *good* and *pleasing* and *perfect*.

(Romans 12:1-2)

DAY 5: INTO THE GRAY

Scripture Focus

Romans 14

One of my favorite musical groups in college was Out of the Grey. They were a husband and wife team who sang contemporary Christian music. Their name makes me think of moving out of apathy or confusion into total devotion for God. Today when we talk about going into the gray, I'm not asking us to compromise our theological positions or move into a lukewarm faith.

All Christians must move into the gray to navigate issues of conscience. These are choices or beliefs that are not black or white for everyone. Today we will find Paul teaching us that some things can be wrong for one person and totally acceptable in God's eyes for another. Some areas aren't sin for everyone and aren't right for all people, so therefore they are gray.

What are some gray areas for us Christians that come to your mind?

politics   Church & state

I know amazing godly people on both sides of the issues when it comes to:

- Traditional or contemporary music styles during worship services
- The frequency and method that Communion is celebrated
- Whether speaking in tongues is still a spiritual gift given today
- Whether or not it is okay to drink alcohol *in moderation*

These are just a few areas where I see Christians clash. I have personal opinions when it comes to these controversial topics, but I wouldn't dig in my heels for any of the views that I hold on these matters. I search the Scriptures, seek counsel, and pray about these things, but I can't say that others who believe differently are definitely wrong.

Some essentials in our faith are not gray. We never compromise when it comes to the gospel message. God loving us, sin creating a barrier to intimacy in our relationship with God, Christ dying and rising again, and our need to personally receive these truths are essentials. At the foot of the cross and beside the empty tomb, we find common ground that unites all Christ-followers. In my experience, most Christians aren't fighting on Facebook about the gospel message. They are often arguing about politics or preferences that fall into gray areas.

In Romans 14, Paul gives us some practical advice in how to handle our differing opinions.

Read Romans 14:1-9, and write below the two examples Paul gives of gray issues during the writing of his letter:

vv. 2-3 *eating meat*

vv. 5-6a *holding a sabbath*

As you read these verses, how would you boil down the core message of Paul's teaching in one sentence?

We should not spend our time & energy judging e/o

Essentially, we are to accept one another and not argue with each other. Can you imagine if this instruction was widely applied in today's churches? How about on social media? This doesn't mean we can't talk about or debate hot topics. We all can mature in wisdom as we share, discuss, and listen to one another. However, we are not to argue. God accepted or valued those who ate or didn't eat certain foods and wanted to honor Him in their decisions (v. 3).

This is a tough topic for me. I like to know the "right" answer and then universally apply it. I know some other people like this, too, and in the New Testament they are the Pharisees. Grace is messier than law. It means that we must accept each other even when we think we are "right" and others are "wrong." It allows us to live in the tension of opposing ideas while genuinely accepting and loving others.

Where is the Lord calling you to accept someone else (who might see things differently than you in some area) right now?

religious music/stuff @ school

Often we disagree because we are so different. God created a variety of personality tendencies. I love the Meyers Briggs, Ennegram, and DISC personality

tests. They help me understand the way God has wired me, as well as help me see others who think, feel, and process differently than I do. In addition to different personalities, our backgrounds are also different.

The Roman church consisted of Jews who grew up with strict moral rules and Gentiles who might have been involved in prostitution or idol worship before they decided to follow Jesus. In the same way, we worship alongside others who did not have the same home life or education that we experienced. My best friend grew up in a home where alcohol was abused. She has a hard time understanding why anyone would want to touch that stuff when the consequences of drunkenness are so costly. I know others who grew up in homes where alcohol was consumed in moderation. Because the Bible only forbids drunkenness, they feel the personal freedom to responsibly enjoy alcohol (without causing harm to anyone else). We have freedom but with the responsibility of considering how our decisions will impact others. If those in both camps prayerfully evaluate and choose, it's possible they might be honoring God while making opposite choices.

At times we can feel so strongly about the way the Lord has led us in a certain area that we assume it is the right choice for everyone else. This can lead us to criticize or judge others. We come by it naturally. Something in our flesh sees our choices as right. Anyone who feels more freedom than we do, we can tag as permissive. Those who choose a stricter view than we hold in a certain area, we tend to label as legalists. Instead, God asks us to get outside of our limited view and see others the way He does.

> **God asks us to get outside of our limited view and see others the way He does.**

Read Romans 14:10-19, and answer the following questions:

What should we refrain from doing to other believers? (vv. 10, 13a)

judging

What does it mean to put a stumbling block in the way of someone? How can we keep from doing this? (v. 13b)

To make things difficult

To whom will we give a personal account? (v. 12)

God

What should we stop doing? (v. 13)

judging others

How is the kingdom of God described? (v. 17)

a place of righteousness, peace & joy in the Holy Spirit

What will happen if you serve Christ with an attitude of goodness, peace, and joy in the Holy Spirit? (v. 18)

We will please God & Others

What should we aim for in the church? (v. 19)

To keep the peace & build %o up

Take a moment to search your heart and mind. Whom have you been critical of in your thoughts and feelings lately? A family member, coworker, person at church, neighbor, or total stranger on social media? Ask the Lord to show you how you can be authentic about your differences with others without tearing down God's work in their lives. Write a short prayer below in response to the verses we've just read:

Father God help me to stop judging and start loving and supporting others more

I don't know if these verses convict you in the same way that they resonate with me. I have battled most of my Christian life with thinking my way is the "right" way. Like the Queen of Hearts in *Alice in Wonderland*, my thoughts and actions reveal a posture like hers that says, "All ways are MY ways." I need God's help to truly accept others who think, feel, or act differently than I do. This has impacted my marriage, friendships, and church relationships as I continue to grow in acceptance and understanding. It is vital that we take these words to heart, especially in our church contexts.

Read Romans 14:20-23 and summarize Paul's final instructions to the Roman church in this chapter:

Do not undo the work of God by letting petty judgements get in the way

Paul says our preferences (whether food or drink or something else) can tear apart the work of God. Have you seen God's mission or message thwarted by church members fighting over nonessentials? If so, share an example of what you've experienced or observed below:

Disagreements over ministers, music, hymnals, schools

What are some ways that we can help restore harmony when these kinds of circumstances arise?

Pray and speak honestly

We can be the ones who speak healing words, refuse to gossip, and bring clarity in determining the differences between biblical absolutes and gray areas. Each follower of Christ has a unique sanctification process. The Holy Spirit works in each person's life as they submit to His leading. When we encounter clear sin in the lives of others, the Lord might lead us to lovingly help them get back on the right path or to pray for them and wait on God. But when others' choices are different in gray areas, we must guard against assuming that what is right for us is right for all. We should evaluate carefully before confronting others to be sure we aren't majoring in the minors of the Christian faith. A widely quoted maxim whose authorship has been debated advises, "In essentials unity, in non-essentials liberty, in all things charity."[18]

Paul says we are blessed when we don't feel guilty for doing something we have decided is right (Romans 14:22). He also says when we do anything we're not sure is right, we are sinning (Romans 14:23). What does this mean for us? We must wrestle with our beliefs when it comes to living the Christian life and be fully convinced of God's leading as we make decisions. However, we must accept that God may lead others down an opposite path. As we've seen today in Romans 14, sometimes we must dive into the gray in order to love others well.

Talk with God

Lord, give me Your eyes and show me where you are leading me when it comes to gray issues in the Christian life. Help me to see clearly what are absolutes for all believers and what might be nonessentials—things that You lead us to view differently. Give me the ability to see outside of my limited views and experiences so that I can accept others who are different than I am. I want to love others the way You do. Amen.

Memory Verse Exercise

Read the Memory Verse on page 136 several times, and then fill in the blanks below as you recite it:

¹And *so*, dear *brothers* and *sisters*, I *plead* with *you* to *give* your *bodies* to *Christ because* of *all* he has *done* for you. Let *them* be a *living* and *holy sacrifice*—the *kind* he *will find acceptable*. This is *truly* the *way to worship* him. ²Don't *copy* the *behavior* and *customs* of this *world*, but *let* God *transform* you *into* a new *person* by *changing* the way you *think*. Then *you* will *learn* to know *Gods will* for you, which is *good* and *pleasing* and *perfect*.

(Romans 12:1-2)

Big Idea

God sometimes gives us different instructions in gray areas and always calls us to accept each other.

Weekly Wrap Up

Review the Big Idea for each day, and then write any personal application that comes to mind.

Day 1: Lasting Change
Big Idea: We continually offer ourselves as living sacrifices and allow God to change us through the renewing of our minds.

Personal Application:_____

_____

Day 2: Bullfrogs and Butterflies
Big Idea: When we allow Christ to transform us by the renewing of our minds, it affects our relationships in incredible ways.

Personal Application:_____
_____

Day 3: Love and Respect
Big Idea: God calls us to honor our governing authorities and to love others.

Personal Application:_____
_____

Day 4: Belief and Behavior
Big Idea: Our belief in Jesus overflows into right behavior.

Personal Application:_____
_____

Day 5: Into the Gray
Big Idea: God sometimes gives us different instructions in gray areas and always calls us to accept each other.

Personal Application:_____
_____

GOOD NEWS ABOUT RELATIONSHIPS

We have to go _____ before _____.

Romans 12:1-2

Romans 12:3

_____ is great for photo booths but bad for relationships.

Romans 12:9-10

Romans 13:8-10

In relationships we are always one choice away from _____.

Romans 14:8-13

Romans 12:3, 16

Romans 14:1, 13

Week 6

Good News About Eternity

Romans
15–16

Memory Verse

The God of peace will soon crush Satan under your feet. May the grace of our Lord Jesus be with you. (Romans 16:20)

DAY 1: HARMONY, HOPE, AND THE HOLY SPIRIT

Scripture Focus

Romans 15:1-13

We've come to the last two chapters in Paul's letter to the Romans and our last week of study. I'm so proud of you for finishing strong. Take a moment to celebrate that you have covered fourteen chapters of Romans!

At times this book has been challenging as we've tried to wrap our minds around hard truths. In other portions we've read powerful gospel truths that I hope have encouraged your socks off. We've found good news that has the power to change everything in our lives:

Good News About Faith—God calls us to believe and accept His free gift of forgiveness through the life and death of Christ.

Good News About Hope—This good news about Christ causes us to maintain a hopeful perspective even in the midst of the difficulties and suffering of this life.

Good News About Daily Life—God has given us His Spirit to help us as He sanctifies us and gives us power over sin.

Good News About God's Plan—We embrace the good news with greater insight as we see that God's plan hasn't changed. He has always invited people to start a relationship with Him by faith, not by obedience or ancestry.

Good News About Relationships—As we offer ourselves as living sacrifices to God and allow Him to transform us by changing the way we think, we are able to bring His grace into our relationships.

This week we will wrap up our study by looking at "Good News About Eternity." The gospel of Christ is not something we check off our list of things to do. We don't say, "Gospel—check. Yep, I believed that when I was...(10, 25, 45, etc.), and I'm all set." The good news about Christ is so much more than a one-time past experience. Paul ends his letter with a series of teachings that reveal the good news about Christ as both a present and future reality, transforming the way we think and live today and tomorrow and echoing into eternity. Remember that we've seen the good news of salvation as threefold:

- Through *justification* God saved us from the *penalty* of sin.
- Through *sanctification* we are being saved from the *power* of sin.

Digging Deeper

As Paul gives his final greetings to the church at Rome, we learn about the structure and affection of the early church. For a deeper look at the early church, check out the Digging Deeper article for Week 6, "Kissing Christians" (see AbingdonWomen.com/Romans).

- One day we will experience *glorification* in heaven, where we will be saved from the *presence* of sin.

Our salvation is good news forever. We begin a relationship with God by believing in Christ's death as the final sacrifice for our sin. After we declare with our mouths that Jesus is Lord and believe in our hearts that God raised Him from the dead, we are never the same. Our past, present, and future take on new freedom and purpose.

This all sounds amazing. So why doesn't life feel free and purposeful every day? Living on a broken planet, we endure incredible hardships. This past year I've had the opportunity to travel across the country and teach from Scripture at events and conferences. After an event, I often get to pray with women. I've heard stories of heartbreaking divorce, the death of loved ones, financial woes, and difficult relationships of all kinds. Whether our bad news is devastating and tragic or a million little things such as sore bodies, distracted minds, parking tickets, and broken dishwashers, we have a sense that life wasn't supposed to be this way.

God created a perfect world, but sin has marred it beyond recognition. So God came down to us in human form. Jesus overcame sin and death through His ultimate sacrifice on the cross. Through His blood we can approach a holy God with confidence. We can cling to this good news in the midst of complicated lives. What good news!

Today we'll find three more pieces of good news as we open Romans 15. We'll see that God longs for us to experience:

- Harmony
- Hope
- His Holy Spirit

The chapter begins with Paul elaborating on gray areas, the topic he discusses in the previous chapter, which we explored yesterday. We see that the Roman Christians seem to be having differing opinions about which foods they should or shouldn't eat and which day is the best to worship God. Paul teaches that believers should consider each other in their decisions.

Read Romans 15:1-13 and answer the following questions:

What should strong (mature) believers do when it comes to weaker (less developed in their faith) believers? (vv. 1-2)

Bear w/them & build them up

What does God help us do that is right for all followers of Christ? (v. 6)

glorify God

What command does Paul repeat that he taught in Romans 14? (v. 7)

live in unity; accept one another

Paul is teaching about harmony, which is a key factor in our reputation as Christians in a secular world. In music, harmony is the blending of different notes in a way that makes a lovely sound. We can look for common ground in the good news about Christ and learn to disagree about minor issues with more love and respect. We can find unity without uniformity. (And we can learn to dialogue more in person rather than use harsh words online to fight!) In our pursuit of sound doctrine we might be tempted to put every issue on level ground, but this can lead to us become passionate about minor issues of mode and method. We never are to compromise the gospel message, but I find more people fighting about which Christian leader has compromised theologically or who Christians should back in an election than about the gospel message of God's love, humanity's sin, Christ's sacrifice, and our need to receive Christ. With an eternal perspective, the gospel takes center stage and we remember what matters most to God. And harmony with one another is high on His list!

> **We can look for common ground in the good news about Christ and learn to disagree about minor issues with more love and respect.**

In what ways do you see your local church family succeeding or struggling with these instructions about harmony in Romans 15?

I think we have come a long way in the last 10 years

Now we've hit a little closer to home. This is where things get personal. Are you helping or criticizing others who are different from you? Maybe you are watching believers harshly fight over gray issues and remaining silent. Perhaps you are claiming superiority because you have been a Christian longer than those you disagree with regarding gray areas. God says you need to be considerate and accepting of those who are weaker or less developed in their faith. The admonitions in these verses are mostly aimed at the mature believer.

What are some practical ways you can take these teachings to heart as you accept other believers who have different opinions than you do?

Try to be more understanding of others' opinions

Paul says we must consider others. This doesn't mean we are held hostage to the weakest believer's opinion on any given topic or that we make decisions that please everyone else. (I've tried that and it never works because you can't win. If you please one person, likely another is upset.) Paul was not a fan of peacekeeping but of peacemaking. He writes in other letters:

> Our purpose is to please God, not people. He alone examines the motives of our hearts.
>
> (1 Thessalonians 2:4b-c)

> Obviously, I'm not trying to win the approval of people, but of God. If pleasing people were my goal, I would not be Christ's servant.
>
> (Galatians 1:10)

Paul is certainly not a people-pleaser. However, he warns us against a very prevalent worldview in our modern society. He says we shouldn't live to please ourselves.

Through commercials, conversations, and billboards we hear messages such as "You do you" and "Have it your way." We need balance when it comes to this self-pleasing versus people-pleasing thing. Instead, like Paul, we need to become God-pleasers. Harmony is important to God, so it should be important to us. We don't want to live under the bondage of others' opinions, but at the same time, the impact of our decisions on others must be a factor.

What is a decision you've been considering lately?

When & where to move

Who will be affected by this decision?

family & friends

Whether you've been thinking about starting a new eating plan or taking a different job, your choices will affect others. While we don't live to please others, we do live to please God. And He says He wants us to think about each other and not cause roadblocks that might negatively impact the faith of others.

A beautiful song can uplift our spirits, and harmony in the church can bring good news to a hurting world.

Let's read Romans 15:1-13 one more time and find two other "H" words that remind us that this good news is for today. Look for mentions of heaven and the Holy Spirit, and then answer the following questions:

What does verse 4 say the Scriptures give us as we wait patiently for God's promises to be fulfilled?

hope

According to verse 13, what will God fill us with?

joy & peach

What will we overflow (or abound) with?

hope

Through what power is this accomplished?

the Holy Spirit

How is this good news for you today in the midst of whatever trials you have been facing recently?

Hope through the power of the Holy Spirit applies to every single one of us. No matter what challenges you are walking through right now, you can rest in hope knowing that good things are ahead—whether in this life or the next. The Holy Spirit resides in us and reminds us of these truths. I hope that you can hear His voice today and that these gospel truths will encourage you now and in the days to come.

Talk with God

Lord, I pray for harmony in the church. Help us to love and accept one another. As I think about my choices today, show me how I can consider others. I can get discouraged

by all that is happening in the world, but remind me of the hope I have in You. Fill me with your Holy Spirit so that I might experience Your power today. Amen.

Memory Verse Exercise

Big Idea

God's good news can bring harmony and hope in our lives through the power of the Holy Spirit.

Read the Memory Verse on page 166 several times, and then fill in the blanks below as you recite it:

The God of _peace_ will soon crush Satan under your _feet_. May the _grace_ of our Lord Jesus be with you.

(Romans 16:20)

DAY 2: GODLY CONFIDENCE

Scripture Focus

Romans 15:14-22

Confidence wouldn't be the word that described me for the bulk of my life. I was a shy and fearful child. I can't say I entered many rooms with confidence during my teen years either. Then when I became a mother, I felt unsure of most of my choices on any given day. Lack of confidence robs us in so many ways. Our indecision, uncertainty, and fear not only can steal our joy but also steer us in wrong directions.

I read many books to prepare for motherhood after I found out I was pregnant with my first child. *What to Expect When You're Expecting* became my good friend on a daily basis. I also read about breastfeeding, sleep training, and so forth. Yet what I lacked was confidence in some of the basic instincts of motherhood. I didn't have any close friends or mentors to encourage me since we were new to a small town in Canada where my husband had his first job as a youth pastor.

I'm going to tell on myself a little bit and give you permission to laugh at my twenty-two-year-old naivety. During the first weeks of my son's life, I really struggled to get the hang of breastfeeding. When my milk finally came in several days after he was born, I was feeding him on one side and found myself getting soaked with milk on the other. My naive mind thought, "Oh, the milk is over there." So I quickly unlatched him and switched sides. I didn't realize that my milk was letting down on both sides. I eventually figured out that just as he was beginning to drink, I had been interrupting his feeding by changing his position.

My lack of knowledge and confidence made feeding my baby much more difficult than it could have been. Perhaps the books I read assumed that moms would instinctively know milk came down on both sides, but this young momma didn't. I can look back and laugh now, grateful that my son managed to survive infancy!

Can you identify a time in your life when you lacked confidence? Describe what comes to mind off the top of your head. (Feel free to make me feel better by writing about any funny stories or situations that resulted.)

Starting a new job
Delivering PD

Maybe you waited too long to apply for a promotion because of insecurities or didn't pursue a friendship because you weren't sure you were good enough. Fear and insecurity are thieves! They stole precious milk from my baby, and they've likely stolen some significant joys from you.

In our study of Romans 15 today, we are going to focus on godly confidence using a three-step process to interact with the passage:

Read the following questions first. Then read Romans 15:14-22 and answer the questions, referring to the text as needed.

What are some of the markers or indicators of confidence we see in Paul's life? (Notice the adjectives and verbs he uses in this section.)

Convinced, they're competent, written you boldly grace God gave me; I glory; power of signs & miracles, power of the spirit

How is confidence different from pride? (vv. 17-18)

Confidence is in Christ, pride is in ourselves

What ambition did Paul have for his ministry? (vv. 20-21)

To preach to those who didn't know Christ

How can we know the difference between prideful ambition and godly goals as we seek to live confidently for Christ?

Pray for wisdom, ask if our actions glorify him

As I thought about these questions, I noticed three key truths about confidence that we can apply in our lives.

1. Confidence comes with the confirmation of God's Word.
2. Confidence comes with encouragement.
3. Confidence comes with clarity.

Let's take some time to explore each of these truths together.

1. Confidence comes with the confirmation of God's Word.

Turn back to Romans 15:4, and summarize this verse in your own words below:

The Scriptures were written to encourage us & give us hope

Paul states that the Scriptures, God's Word, were written to teach us and bring us hope. As we've discussed previously, Paul is referring to the Hebrew Scriptures when he speaks of the Scriptures, because the New Testament books were still being written. Of course, God's Word doesn't give instructions on things such as breastfeeding; but as I've been reading and studying the Bible for the last three decades, I've come to know God better. In its pages I see His character, love, and desire for relationship with us.

What are some of the things you've learned about God from our study of Romans that could bring someone confidence?

We all have gifts — Life is messy now but we have an incredible future

Our lists could be long and different because there is so much insight in Paul's letter. I thought about how there is no condemnation for those who follow Christ (Romans 8:1) and how Christ died for me while I was still a sinner (Romans 5:8), truths that give me confidence in knowing I have value that's not based on my performance. As I know God better, I gain confidence through His love. Another benefit I've noticed from growing in my understanding of God through His Word has been my personal transformation from an insecure child to a more confident daughter of the King.

Godly confidence that is rooted in Scripture isn't arrogant because we realize our source of worth. Paul says in Romans 15:18 that he isn't boasting in himself but in what Christ is doing through Him. We must be careful not to confuse humility with insecurity. Humility recognizes our need for Christ and leans into Him for the power to carry out His mission in our lives. Insecurity shrinks back from opportunities out of a lack of assurance. When we study the Bible, we grow in confidence in God's power to work through us to do mighty things we could never do in our own strength.

How have you noticed a correlation between your study of God's Word and your confidence in general?

I know that even when I fail, he loves me

> **Godly confidence that is rooted in Scripture isn't arrogant because we realize our source of worth.**

We may or may not be able to nail down specific examples, but we can reflect and notice our thoughts, attitudes, and actions changing as we grow in faith through the hearing of God's Word. In the Scriptures we find that we are valuable and gifted by God to accomplish meaningful goals. We also notice that we can encourage others to help them in their battle with insecurity. This brings us to our second key truth about confidence.

2. Confidence comes with encouragement.

In Romans 15:14, Paul tells the believers at Rome that he is convinced they know the good news and are able to teach others. Paul uses words such as *enthusiastic* and *convinced* to bolster the church's confidence. He encourages them with reminders of the truth.

Don't we need reminders too? Life can be downright depressing. Recently some of my sweet friends and ministry partners were talking about the need to remind each other of God's hope for eternity. One of them lost her brother this year as he was serving our country overseas. Another was mediating a conflict between her grown children over the phone. Some days the brokenness of our planet affects us deeply, and we need to be reminded that we have a future and a hope.

Paul complimented the believers with tangible statements such as these:

- You are full of goodness. (Romans 15:14)
- You know these things so well. (Romans 15:14)

We also need encouragement. When I first began writing Bible studies, my lack of confidence screamed, "Who do you think you are? No one wants to read what you have to say! More Bible studies for women aren't needed!"

But encouragement brought confidence as I shared my work first with my own Bible study group and eventually with an editor. A few individuals used these letters in my life:

I C N U   (I see in you)

They said, "ICNU the diligence to study hard." "ICNU the ability to tell stories that relate to the passage." I can't tell you the value of those comments for my confidence. I hope that today you will be the one to give some ICNU statements to others as the Holy Spirit leads you!

Ask God to bring someone to mind who might need encouragement. Write their name below and consider the following questions.

What encouraging words can you say about what this person is doing well right now?

While you don't want to preach at them with trite phrases or Christian clichés, is there a reminder of God's love that you can share this week, either in word or in deed?

If the Lord gives you any action steps, please take a moment now to remind yourself to follow through. Set an alarm on your phone for later today, write a note in your planner or to-do list, or send a quick text now with some words of blessing!

Now, let's focus on our last truth about godly confidence in today's passage.

3. Confidence comes with clarity.

Take a moment to review Romans 15:19-22, and summarize how Paul describes his calling from God:

He was called through the power of the spirit & God's miracles

Paul knew that God wanted him to share the good news about Christ in areas where no church existed yet. He had a passion to plant churches. Once he started a church, others needed to use their gifts to preach and shepherd the church. Earlier in Romans Paul wrote about spiritual gifts, acknowledging that we are not the same. Perhaps you are raising children, nursing sick patients, taking care of an elderly parent, working on staff at a church, or doing something else to use your gifts to honor God and serve others. As you pray, study God's Word, seek encouragement from others, and wrestle with God's Holy Spirit, He gives clarity and opens and closes doors of opportunity to guide you. Without clarity we lack confidence. If we aren't taking the time to seek God about how we are living, we might serve half-heartedly and be unsure of whether we are really making a difference.

When we clearly know God wants us to disciple teenagers, invest in young moms, or clean floors to earn money to support our family, we can feel confident like Paul. He was sure he was doing what God wanted Him to do, which allowed him to worry less about meeting the expectations of others and more about knowing and pursuing God's will with action.

Recall or look up last week's memory verse from Romans 12:1-2. What will result in us knowing God's good, pleasing, and perfect will in our lives? *Letting God transform you into a new person*

As we allow God to transform us by changing the way we think, He will give us clarity. Where is God calling you to serve Him at this stage in your life? *financially helping others*

If you aren't sure how to answer that question, keep asking God for clarity! Pray, study Scripture, seek counsel, and allow God to renew your mind. With greater clarity will come greater confidence!

Talk with God

Lord, I pray that You would give me godly confidence and help me to find that confidence today in You. Give me boldness as I read Your Word and see myself the way You see me. I ask for confirmation from others as I pursue You with a whole heart, trusting that I will have clarity as Your Spirit leads me. Amen.

Memory Verse Exercise

Read the Memory Verse on page 166 several times, and then fill in the blanks below as you recite it:

The God of *peace* will soon *crush* Satan under your *feet*. May the *grace* of our Lord *God* be with you.

(Romans 16:20)

Big Idea

We can grow in godly confidence through our study of God's Word, encouragement from others, and clarity in how to use our time and talents to honor the Lord.

DAY 3: TRAVEL PLANS AND PRAYERS

One of the reasons I don't like surprises is that I find joy in making plans. My husband and I planned for years to take our children on a trip out west. We determined the best year to go based on the kids' ages so that everyone would

be able to hike and endure long car trips with the least amount of whining possible. I called one year to the day to reserve cabins in some of the national parks. My sister's and mentor's families ended up joining us on the adventure.

One of my struggles and joys on the trip was when things didn't go according to the carefully laid plans my sister and I had constructed. I struggled because I like to stick with my schedule. I don't want to miss anything. But I found on this trip that some of our greatest memories came when we had to make a Plan B. The place we went in Yellowstone Park to boat on a lake was too windy for sailing when we arrived. We had driven a long way, and everyone was grumpy. It was there we encountered a restaurant that was one of the highlights of the trip. On the way home we found a lookout point with some of the most breathtaking views I've ever seen. I hadn't read about this place, but our pictures there still make me smile with delight.

Do you like to make plans? How do you respond when your plans get derailed? Yesterday we learned from the apostle Paul about godly confidence. Today we will see that Paul liked to make plans too, and he shared his ideas with the Roman church. With the benefit of hindsight, we know that not all of the things he shared in his letter to the Romans ended up according to plan. It reminds me of Proverbs 16:9: "We can make our plans, / but the LORD determines our steps."

How have you found this verse to prove true in your life? Can you give an example of a time when God determined different steps than the plans you had made?

What I thought my long-term plan might be in college

There was a guy I thought I was going to marry, but I didn't. I made plans for one baby during pregnancy and found out ten days before birth that I was carrying twins. I wanted to sail around Yellowstone Lake in boats, but instead I sat in a fancy restaurant in my swimsuit cover-up eating delicious food as I looked out over that lake.

Let's see what plans Paul made. Read Romans 15:23-33, and label the following statements as True (T) or False (F) according to the plans he shares in these verses:

_F_ 1. I have finished my work in other places, and now I am planning to visit you in Rome. (v. 23)

_F_ 2. I am planning to go to Egypt and will stop off in Rome. (v. 24)

F 3. After we have a good visit, I am hoping that you will help pay for the rest of my trip. (v. 24)

F 4. Before I come, I need to take an offering from the believers in Ethiopia to the church in Jerusalem. (vv. 25-26)

T 5. As soon as I have delivered this money in Jerusalem, I will come to visit you. (v. 28)

F 6. I'm sure that when I come, we will fight. (v. 29)

T 7. I hope that you will join in my struggle by praying for me. (v. 30)

Okay, so Paul wasn't planning to go to Egypt; he was headed for Spain. And the offering for Jerusalem was from the believers in Macedonia and Achaia, not Ethiopia. He also wasn't planning to fight with the Roman church but hoped that Christ would richly bless their time together. Everything else was true!

Are you wondering which of these things actually turned out the way Paul had planned? I know my inquiring mind wants to know. According to Acts 21, several people on Paul's journey prophesied that he should not go to Jerusalem (v. 4); another said that if he did, he would be imprisoned (v. 11). But Paul went to Jerusalem anyway. When some Jews saw him in the temple, a riot broke out (Acts 21:30). Roman soldiers got involved, and Paul lived through a series of circumstances that were not part of the plan that we read in his letter to the Romans.

Here's what happened to Paul:

- He was almost whipped by Roman soldiers until he told them he was a Roman citizen (Acts 22:24-29).
- He had a dream from the Lord telling him not to be afraid because he would share the good news in Rome eventually (Acts 23:11).
- He was sent to Rome as a prisoner aboard a ship that encountered a storm, leaving him shipwrecked on the Island of Malta (Acts 27).
- He suffered a snake bite that didn't harm him so that the people of Malta thought he was a god (Acts 28:1-10).
- He finally arrived at Rome and lived under house arrest as a prisoner for two years where he boldly preached the good news (Acts 28:11-31).

These weren't exactly the plans Paul wrote about in his Letter to the Romans. He didn't plan to come to Rome in chains, be shipwrecked, or have an encounter with a snake. We don't know if he ever even made it to Spain. A few commentators mention a reference in the first letter of Clement, an anonymous letter (traditionally attributed to Pope Clement) written to the church in Corinth

in the late first century AD, which says Paul reached the "farthest limits of the west," which likely referred to his mission in Spain.[1] Others would not make this conclusion because the absence of evidence of Paul's missionary work could lead us to believe that trip never took place.[2] This recalls another Proverb. "You can make many plans, / but the Lord's purpose will prevail" (Proverbs 19:21).

One commentator explains it like this:

> God allowed Paul to dream of Spain in order that he might write Romans. No matter that Paul probably never reached Spain. What mattered was that he wrote this letter, which has been far more powerful and influential than any missionary visit, even by Paul himself, could ever have been. Perhaps...half our great plans, the dreams we dream for our churches and our world, and even for ourselves, are dreams God allows us to dream in order that, on the way there, we may accomplish, almost without realizing it, the crucial thing God intends us to do.[3]

I have found this to be true in so many different areas of life. As I have planned to go in one direction, I've found new dreams or purposes even when things shifted direction in my life. When I started writing, the idea of public speaking was daunting because of my shyness. Yet God ended up calling me to teach. I've found that I am still scared but enjoy sharing what I'm learning in my studies that might relate to others in a helpful way.

Someone once said to me, "God directs a moving car." While I can't find chapter and verse for this statement, I've found that often as we step out and begin to risk and adventure with the Lord, God directs us as we move with Him.

What are some plans you are making for your next week, month, and year? I've written my own responses to encourage you to share yours.

Next week:
I hope to finish a writing project in the next week before my college kids return for a holiday school break.

Next month:
I plan to rest and read some fiction just for fun after having spent many hours with my nose in commentaries.

Next year:

*This is more difficult; I'm not good at planning too far out. My dream
would be to write another Bible study, move into the house we are
currently building, and follow God down new paths as He leads.*

*Move more forward make a decision
about moving*

I don't know what plans you have in front of you as we near the end of our
Romans study. If you have small children at home, I pray you have intentional
plans to disciple them in the ways of Christ. Maybe at work you plan to bring
the light of Jesus through your smile and warmth and wisdom. Perhaps you are
caring for an aging loved one and plan to love and serve them well even when
you are weary.

Paul made plans confidently. We don't know whether he had complete
peace when his plans were derailed or he struggled to reconcile the changes. I
learn from this passage that I can dream big and even tell others about my plans
but ultimately rest in God's ability to direct. This means I hold my plans loosely,
allowing God to course-correct when needed.

We also know that Paul prayed over his plans and enlisted others to pray
alongside him.

**Look again at Romans 15:30-33, and write below some of the specific
things Paul asked the church at Rome to pray for him:**

*to be rescued from unbelievers
to serve acceptably
come to them in joy) to be refreshed*

Paul asked them to join in his struggle by praying. He prayed for rescue but
was imprisoned. He prayed that the church in Jerusalem would accept his gift,
and they did. He prayed that he would be able to come to Rome with a joyful
heart and be an encouragement; and even though he was under house arrest,
Acts 28 reveals Paul had a powerful ministry in Rome. Then at the end of his
prayer in Romans 15, Paul wrote these words: "And now may God, who gives us
his peace, be with you all" (v. 33).

Whatever plans you are making, know that sometimes God will direct in
different ways. Things likely won't turn out exactly the way you thought they
would. They certainly didn't for the apostle Paul! Yet if we fall in step with God's
Spirit, we can pray for God's peace and presence as we make our plans and trust
the Lord to direct our steps.

**We can pray
for God's peace
and presence
as we make
our plans
and trust the
Lord to direct
our steps.**

Talk with God

Lord, help me as I make plans. Give me dreams of more people hearing about Your love. Use my gifts and talents in ways that honor You. When You change the plans I've laid out, help me to be flexible. Show me that Your plans are always higher than mine. I long to know Your good and pleasing and perfect will. Amen.

Memory Verse Exercise

Read the Memory Verse on page 166 several times, and then fill in the blanks below as you recite it:

The _God_ of _peace_ will soon _crush_ Satan _under_ your _feet_. May the _grace_ of our Lord _Jesus_ be with _you_

Romans 16:20

Big Idea

We make plans, but God directs our steps.

DAY 4: SPIRITUAL FRIENDS

Scripture Focus

Romans 16:1-16

Extra Insight

After doing an in-depth study of the names in Romans 16, the historian Peter Lampe found that a majority of the names Paul mentioned were those belonging to Gentiles, freedmen who had previously been slaves, or descendants of slaves and freedmen. This helps us understand the social makeup of the early church and gives us context regarding Paul's intended audience.[4]

The Wizard of Oz was shown on television once a year when I was a child. My siblings and I would be excited for this special night and enjoyed watching Dorothy and her friends on their quest to have their wishes granted. After videotapes and then DVDs became available, we could have watched this movie anytime, but we never did anymore.

Do you have any similar stories of shows you watch less now that they are more readily available with technology?

Many holiday things

Some of you may not remember a time before VCRs, DVRs, or Netflix, but for me something about The Wizard of Oz being a rare opportunity made it special. I find this happens in other areas of life too. When we can do something anytime, we might not prioritize it.

Communication in Paul's day was limited to handwritten letters, and so personal greetings in letters were important. Paul took the time to write intentionally and included personal greetings to his friends and ministry partners who worshiped with the body of believers in Rome. Even though he had never been there, he knew many individuals through his ministry travels.

As we talk about good news for eternity in this last week of our study, talking about people is appropriate. Only two things will last forever: the Word of God and the souls of people. I wish I wrote more letters and expressed my appreciation for the people the Lord has placed in my life more often. An array of communication options is available to me. I can email, text, call, use social media messaging, as well as write letters and talk in person. For me it can be a little bit like watching *The Wizard of Oz* after it became readily available. Once I can do it anytime, I struggle to make it a priority at all. Paul took the time to connect personally. Greetings at the end of his letters to churches were common for Paul, but the length of his comments in the Roman letter is substantial. Here his greetings are more than double the length of those in his other letters.

As an introvert, I admire Paul's breadth of meaningful relationships. He greeted twenty-six individuals, two families, and three house churches. He seemed to know so many people. He wasn't just a church leader but a sincere friend-maker.

Read Romans 16:1-16, and record below just two of the many personal comments Paul made to his spiritual friends in Rome:

Person Named	How Paul knew them	Personal comment
Phoebe	Church in Cenchrea	She was a great help to many
Andronicus Junias	prison	Outstanding apostles

What stood out to you as you read Paul's greetings?

The number of people who were working so hard to spread the gospel

While there is some debate of the gender of some names, I couldn't help but notice the amount of women Paul mentioned. Of the possible ten women named, six are commended for their ministry: Phoebe, Priscilla, Junias, Tryphena, Tryphosa, and Persis.

Paul takes the time to thoughtfully greet and encourage people in his life. As we near the end of our study, would you join me in being intentional about encouraging those God has placed in our own lives? Don't skip this part and figure you can do it later, because it might end up being like *The Wizard of Oz* is for me!

For each of the four categories below, write the first name that comes to mind after reading the description. Then take a moment to send a quick greeting telling the person how you value them. Whether you use your phone, computer, or a letter with an envelope and stamp, express your thanks. Record the method you use.

Identify someone who has been a Phoebe in your life—a church leader who is worthy of honor and has been helpful to you:

Name	Method of greeting

Identify someone who has been like Priscilla and Aquila to you—a co-worker or peer who has a similar position in life and a similar heart for ministry: (Priscilla and Aquila were tent-makers like Paul.)

Name	Method of greeting
Patty	phone

Identify someone who is an Epernetus—a dear friend:

Name	Method of greeting
Michele	text

Identify someone who is like Rufus's mother—someone who isn't your biological mother but has been like a mother in your life:

Name	Method of greeting
Arlene	

Whether this exercise made you grateful for the many people God has placed in your life or revealed a lack of godly friends and mentors, Paul is reminding us that relationships are valuable.

Read the following verses and underline the words *friend* and *friends*:

The seeds of good deeds become a tree of life;
   a wise person wins friends.

(Proverbs 11:30)

There are "friends" who destroy each other,
    but a real friend sticks closer than a brother.
                    (Proverbs 18:24)

As iron sharpens iron,
    so a friend sharpens a friend.
                    (Proverbs 27:17)

What is a practical way you can be intentional in investing in friendships this week?

Reaching out more

After moving to a new town recently, being the new girl has meant either being proactive in making friends or sitting home alone. Here are some ideas I've been thinking about as I've been contemplating investing in new friendships:

- Invite a few people over to get to know each other better with a game or a question that helps people connect.
- Reach out to someone you think could be a "sharpening" friend and pursue them. Invite them to meet for lunch, coffee, or a walk.
- Join a small group or serving team at your church in order to see who is like-minded and fun to be around.

You may already enjoy many long-time spiritual friendships, but none of us has ever met our friend quota. Paul was on the lookout to welcome people. With our transient society, there are new people in your church, neighborhood, schools, and workplace. If we have established closed circles, then we leave no room for those in need of community.

It can be easier to spend more time watching the lives of others through screens than putting yourself out there in real, messy relationships. But Paul showed that the good news is meant to be lived out in community. He shared the gospel with those who didn't know Christ but also reminded the Roman Christians of how the good news impacted them in their daily walk.

Believers can "gospelize" each other regularly. I've been hearing this word lately. What does it look like in real life to *gospelize* each other? It simply means to help each other apply the gospel in our everyday situations.

Let's choose selfishness as an area in my life where I need the help of my spiritual friends to gospelize me. My desire is to put Christ first and honor others above myself, yet so many times I put myself first and want things my way. When I have talked with a godly friend or mentor about my battle with selfishness, they have encouraged me by reminding me of gospel truths—truths that connect with the themes of justification, sanctification, and glorification we've studied previously:

Justification—There is no condemnation for those in Christ (Romans 8:1). Jesus paid the penalty for my sin on the cross. When I remember this, guilt and shame have no power over me.

Sanctification—Every believer still struggles with the power of sin. We will never be sinless here on earth, but with God's help we can sin less. When I admit my selfishness and cling to God, He can transform me into a new person by changing the way I think.

Glorification—Though we are still fighting the battle with sin, one day we will be saved from the very presence of sin. We can remind each other that our battle with sin has an expiration date and we know who wins the war.

This is just one example of how we can gospelize each other. As we walk alongside others in faith, we can remind each other of gospel truths and how they apply in our struggles with sin, relationships, soul care, and every area of life.

Dorothy had to go to Oz to realize how grateful she was for the people she loved in Kansas. Oz was colorful and exciting, but Kansas was real. We live in a culture in danger of spending more time in the curated world of online personas rather than developing authentic spiritual friendships. Paul shows us that relationships enriched his life. Even though people can be complicated at times, the good news that changes everything includes intentional friendships.

Talk with God

Lord, give me eyes to see the spiritual friends You have given me. Help me to be a friend-maker and encourager of others. Jesus, show me how to be intentional and set time aside to appreciate the people You have put in my life. Amen.

Memory Verse Exercise

Read the Memory Verse on page 166 several times, and then fill in the blanks below as you recite it:

The _God_ of _peace_ will soon _crush satan under_ your _but_. May the _God_ of our _Lord Jesus_ be with _you_ _Grace_

(Romans 16:20)

Even though people can be complicated at times, the good news that changes everything includes intentional friendships.

Big Idea

God's good news that changes everything includes investing our lives in a community of spiritual friends.

DAY 5: VICTORY

Scripture Focus

Romans 16:17-27

I'll just go ahead and admit it: I like winning. Our family plays a lot of board games, and I play to win every time. Of course, I try to be a good sport when someone else wins, but victory just feels good.

Is there something you like to win at? Name something that just feels good to win:

> *Slots, even though I never play trivia*

Of course, not every activity has a winner; but when the sports team we follow comes out on top or we get the highest score in anything from bridge to bowling, it lifts our spirits.

In our battle with sin, we experience seasons of victory and other times when we feel defeated. When it comes to our spiritual lives, we must remember that we fight from a position of victory. Though we get discouraged when we give in to temptation and use unkind words, act selfishly, or make unwise choices, God wants us to admit our sin and turn toward Him continually as He sanctifies us and matures us. We have so much hope even in the midst of our failings. In Paul's final words to the church at Rome, he reminds the church of the victory we have in the good news.

Read Romans 16:17-20, and summarize Paul's final appeal and encouragement to the church:

Appeal (vv. 17-18)

> *Watch out for people who smooth talk & put obstacles in our way*

Encouragement (vv. 19-20)

> *God is going to crush satan*

Paul warns the church that this good news can get twisted. He tells us to watch out for people causing division, serving their own interests and using smooth talk and glowing words to deceive. So Paul appeals to the church to watch out for those who try to change the clear, simple gospel message. The good news should not get buried, distorted, or changed in any way. This is why we need spiritual friends to gospelize each other when we get off course.

Now that we have studied Romans, how would you summarize the gospel message in a few sentences? (If you need help, look back at Romans 5:8.)

Christ died for us and we can rejoice in justification, sanctification and glorification

God loves us. Our sin separated us from intimacy with God, but Christ died to restore our relationship with Him. When we confess this with our mouths and believe it in our hearts, God saves us from:

- the penalty of sin (justification)
- the power of sin (sanctification)
- and eventually the very presence of sin (glorification)

We cannot add or subtract anything from this good news. Even though Paul warns the church about people doing this, we know that ultimately our enemies are not merely human. As Paul writes to the church at Ephesus, "For we are not fighting against flesh-and-blood enemies, but against evil rulers and authorities of the unseen world, against mighty powers in this dark world, and against evil spirits in the heavenly places" (Ephesians 6:12).

The God of peace will soon crush Satan under your feet. May the grace of our Lord Jesus be with you.
(Romans 16:20)

Read Romans 16:20 in the margin. Whom does Paul say will be crushed?

Satan

What word is used to describe God in this verse?

peace

He is the God of peace, and soon He will crush Satan underneath our feet.

Once when I spoke at an event, I received a goody bag full of trinkets. Typically I have brought these thoughtful gestures home for my daughters. One of the things they loved most was pencils that said "Not today, Satan." We had never heard that expression before. They began using those pencils at school and putting pictures of them on their social media. I noticed recently when one of my girls was home on a college break that she had purchased a sticker for her laptop with those three words so that she would see them every day.

I believe "Not today, Satan" resonates because every day doesn't feel like a victory. Sometimes it seems like the enemy is winning. We can feel hopeless, discouraged, and downright defeated. Many times it is suffering and sin that get us down. Other times I don't even have a good reason for it; life just doesn't feel victorious. That's when we can gospelize each other and say, "Not today, Satan!"

Let's remember that the God of peace will soon crush him under our feet. The apostle John wrote this truth, "But you belong to God, my dear children. You have already won a victory over those people, because the Spirit who lives in you is greater than the spirit who lives in the world" (1 John 4:4). We fight our battle with sin from a position of victory. Although we are not yet free from the *presence* of sin in our lives, God has already paid the penalty for our sin and has set us free from its *power* or control.

How does the reminder that the God of peace will crush Satan under your feet encourage you as you think about the battles you are facing today?

No trial in this world compares to that good news

Remember that you fight from victory. That is some good news!

Now, let's finish Romans by reading 16:21-27. Write in your own words what Paul says in verse 27:

God alone deserves all glory

Paul gives glory to the only wise God. Take a moment to write a prayer giving glory to God for how His good news in Romans has impacted your life over the course of this study:

Father God, thank you so much for justifying me and for never giving up on my sanctification. I pray that every day I may be a little more deserving.

We want to let these truths sink deep, so instead of a Weekly Wrap Up, let's end our study by reviewing what we have learned throughout our weeks together.

> **We fight our battle with sin from a position of victory.**

Read through the main themes in the summary chart, and then draw a star beside the week that resonates most strongly with you during this season of your life. (Don't worry about the reflection questions yet, we will get to those later.)

Week of Study	Main Themes	Reflection Questions
1. Good News About Faith (Romans 1–3)	1. Through faith in Christ we receive God's power! 2. God reveals Himself through creation and invites us to follow His way rather than give in to sinful desires. 3. In the secret places of our hearts and minds we invite Christ to help us view others, ourselves, and God correctly. 4. God's law helps us take a look, give up, and get real as we seek to understand the good news about faith. 5. While we find bad news in sin's power to separate us from God, we rejoice that Christ died to satisfy the penalty of sin and bring us back into fellowship with God.	How are you experiencing God's power in your life right now? How have you seen God revealing Himself to you through His creation and His Word lately? Where have you found yourself categorizing others with an "us" against "them" mentality? How can you bring unity rather than division within the body of believers where you worship? How is God reminding you to stop trying harder in battling sin and, instead, start leaning into Him by faith? Where do you need to take a look, give up, and get real? How have you seen real change in your life as the result of your faith in Christ?

Week of Study	Main Themes	Reflection Questions
2. Good News About Hope (Romans 4–5)	1. We find hope by being connected to a larger family of faith as children of Abraham. 2. Even when our circumstances are puzzling, we can still place our hope in God knowing He fulfills every promise He makes. 3. Though many things in life disappoint us, God's hope never will if we believe and receive it. 4. Christ died for us and wants us not to work for Him but to allow Him to work through us. 5. Adam brought condemnation for everyone but Christ brought a right relationship with God.	Who are some people the Lord has placed in your life who bring you hope? What circumstances have been stealing your hope lately? How has your relationship with the Lord brought hope even in the midst of difficulties? Where do you need to tap in to Christ's power for daily living (in other words, how can you stop living for God and allow God to live through you)? How does seeing Christ as the second Adam who rescues us from sin encourage you today?

Week of Study	Main Themes	Reflection Questions
3. Good News About Daily Life (Romans 6–8)	1. God has given us power over sin and calls us to walk daily in that truth by faith. 2. We need a clear understanding of the purpose of God's law so that we don't veer to the side of legalism or license as we follow Jesus daily. 3. Though we still struggle with sin, God doesn't condemn us and gives us power through His Spirit to overcome sin. 4. We don't have to do what the flesh or sinful nature demands; we can surrender control to the Holy Spirit, which leads to life and peace and pleasing God. 5. The hope of heaven, the Holy Spirit, and the love of God provide good news to help us navigate the daily struggles of life.	Where do you need God's power over persistent sins in your life? Is your personal bent more toward grace or truth? How have you struggled with legalism and license? As you realize that God never condemns you, what shame do you need to release so that you can be free in grace today? How can you yield more fully to God's Holy Spirit right now so that you stop giving in to the demands of your sinful nature? What situations are you going through that cause you to need reminders of the good news of the hope of heaven, the Holy Spirit, and the love of God?

Week of Study	Main Themes	Reflection Questions
4. Good News About God's Plan (Romans 9–11)	1. God blesses and calls His people and invites us to trust His plan. 2. We are not saved by the law but by declaring with our mouths and believing in our hearts the good news about Christ. 3. Faith com... hearing G... Word. 4. God's salvatio... plan includes a diverse family of all who believe and trust in Him. 5. We can't understand all of God's mysterious plans, but we can trust Him to be faithful, gracious, and merciful.	How are you doing right now in trusting God's plan for your life? What did you learn through Romans about trusting the bigger picture of God's plan for all people rather than focusing on your individual frustrations ...omforts? ... you first ...th your ...believe in ...e good ...rist, ...g ...? ...word, ...your Bible study plan after you finish Romans? Where is the Lord calling you to trust Him in the midst of some puzzling or mysterious plans in your life?

Romans 13:1-7

Week of Study	Main Themes	Reflection Questions
5. Good News About Relationships (Romans 12–14)	1. We continually offer ourselves as living sacrifices and allow God to change us through the renewing of our minds.	How is the Lord calling you to offer your life as a living sacrifice right now? Is there a practice or possession you need to lay on the altar?
	2. When we allow Christ to transform us by the renewing of our minds, it affects our relationships in incredible ways.	What have you been allowing into your mind through your eyes and ears lately? How can you intentionally renew your mind so that Christ can transform you into a new person by changing the way you think?
	3. God calls us to honor our governing authorities and to love others.	Which government officials can you lift up in prayer today?
	4. Our belief in Jesus overflows into right behavior.	How have you seen your beliefs impact your behavior over the course of our study?
	5. God sometimes gives us different instructions in gray areas and always calls us to accept each other.	As you think about someone who disagrees with you in a gray area of Scripture, how can you show love and acceptance toward that person in a tangible way this week?

Week of Study	Main Themes	Reflection Questions
6. Good News About Eternity (Romans 15–16)	1. God's good news can bring harmony and hope in our lives through the power of the Holy Spirit. 2. We can grow in godly confidence through our study of God's Word, encouragement from others, and clarity in how to use our time and talents to honor the Lord. 3. We make plans, but God directs our steps. 4. God's good news that changes everything includes investing our lives in a community of spiritual friends. 5. God longs to give us eyes to see His victory and walk in it.	How has the good news recorded in Romans brought you lasting hope? Where is the Lord asking you to grow in confidence? How have you seen God directing your steps as plans have changed in your life? What spiritual friends has the Lord provided for you? What spiritual friends do you need to pursue and invest in more purposefully? How does the message of victory resonate in your life today?

How do the themes of the week that you starred echo into your current circumstances?

Now write a few brief responses to the reflection questions listed for that week (right column of the chart):

The good news about Christ will endure forever. I don't know if your season of study has been one of relative calm or filled with difficulties. Likely you have received some bad news over the course of our study. In the midst of whatever circumstances you find yourself in today, I pray that the good news of Jesus continues to change everything in your life. I hope that the truths you've studied will be hidden in your heart for years to come and that you will see the implications in your faith, hope, daily life, plans, and relationships—and that this good news will echo into eternity as you share it with others.

God longs to give us eyes to see His victory and walk in it.

God longs to give us eyes to see His victory and walk in it. Everything may seem to be going wrong in our world, but we have good news that lasts forever. Christ came and died for us. He rose again and sent His Spirit to help us live victoriously. There is no condemnation for us, and we don't have to do what the flesh or our sinful nature calls us to do. Our hope only intensifies as we realize that the God of peace will soon crush our enemy underneath our feet. This is good news with the power to change *everything* in our lives—we just need to believe it!

Talk with God

Lord, thank You for Your justification and sanctification—and for the promise that one day we will fully understand glorification in Your presence. Help me to believe You more. Thank You for good news for today and every day. Lord, You know I am prone to forget. You know I can become a slave to feelings. I ask You to help me. May our spiritual community realign each of us to the greatness of the news that You loved us enough to send Your Son. Give us all power over sin, and transform us continually through the renewing of our minds. Amen.

Memory Verse Exercise

Read the Memory Verse on page 166 several times, and then fill in the blanks below as you recite it:

The _____ of _____ will _____ _____ _____ _____ your _____. _____ the _____ ___ our _____ _____ be _____ _____.

(Romans 16:20)

Big Idea

God longs to give us eyes to see His victory and walk in it.

GOOD NEWS ABOUT ETERNITY

Suffering has an _____ _____.

Romans 16:20

1 John 4:4

Look for hope in the _____ _____.

Romans 15:4-6, 13

Value _____ above _____.

Romans 16:25-27

VIDEO VIEWER GUIDE ANSWERS

Week 1
trying / trusting
managed / suffering
kindness

Week 2
hope / Savior
God / said
Trials

Week 3
freedom / authority
struggle
godly / God
perspective

Week 4
sovereign plan
gospel
share

Week 5
vertical / horizontal
Posing
honor

Week 6
expiration date
right place
people / stuff

Notes

Introduction to This Study

1. Martin Luther, "Preface to the Letter of Saint Paul to the Romans," in *Luther's Works* 35 (Saint Louis: Concordia, 1960), 365.
2. Warren Wiersbe, *Be Right: How to Be Right with God, Yourself, and Others* (Colorado Springs: David C. Cook, 2008), 13.
3. C. Marvin Pate, *Romans: Teach the Text Commentary Series* (Grand Rapids: Baker Books, 2013), 1.

Introductory Background

1. John R. W. Stott, *The Message of Romans* (Downers Grove, IL: InterVarsity, 1994), 32.
2. Pate, 8.
3. Stott, 25.
4. Frank E. Gaebelein, ed., *The Expositor's Bible Commentary, Volume 10: Romans, 1 Corinthians, 2 Corinthians, Galatians* (Grand Rapids: Zondervan, 1976), 7.
5. Wiersbe, 13.
6. Pate, 13.
7. Douglas J. Moo, *The NIV Application Commentary: Romans* (Grand Rapids: Zondervan, 2000), 25-26.
8. Pate, 10.
9. Charles R. Swindoll, *Swindoll's New Testament Insights: Insights on Romans* (Grand Rapids: Zondervan, 2010), 19.
10. Swindoll, 19.
11. Stott, quoting Martin Luther, 19.
12. Pate, 1.
13. Stott, 11.
14. Alan F. Johnson, quoting Bruce Metzger, *Romans, Volume 1 The Freedom Letter: Everyman's Bible Commentary*, rev. ed. (Chicago: Moody, 1984), 8.
15. Pate, xi.

Week 1: Good News About Faith

1. "Epistle," Dictionary.com, https://www.dictionary.com/browse/epistle?s=t.
2. Carl R. Holladay, A *Critical Introduction to the New Testament: Interpreting the Message and Meaning of Jesus Christ* (Nashville, TN: Abingdon Press, 2005), 280.
3. Pate, 8.
4. "What Does the Term 'Gospel' Mean?," Bible.org, https://bible.org/question/what-does -term-"gospel"-mean.
5. Pate, 16.
6. Pate, 10
7. Swindoll, 15.
8. Strong's 4102, s.v. "pistis," BibleStudyTools.com, https://www.biblestudytools.com /lexicons/greek/kjv/pistis.html.
9. Strong's 1411, s.v. "dunamis," BibleStudyTools.com, https://www.biblestudytools.com /lexicons/greek/kjv/dunamis.html.
10. Wiersbe, 45.
11. "Reconciliation," Baker's Evangelical Dictionary of Biblical Theology, BibleStudyTools .com, https://www.biblestudytools.com/dictionaries/bakers-evangelical-dictionary /reconciliation.html.
12. Wiersbe, 45.
13. "Redeem, Redemption," Baker's Evangelical Dictionary of Biblical Theology, BibleStudyTools.com, https://www.biblestudytools.com/dictionaries/bakers -evangelical-dictionary/redeem-redemption.html.
14. Gaebelein, 19.
15. Moo, 60.
16. Strong's 3860, s.v. "paradidomi," BibleStudyTools.com, https://www.biblestudytools .com/lexicons/greek/kjv/paradidomi.html.
17. Moo, 65.
18. Pate, 9.
19. Johnson, 12.
20. Michael F. Bird, *The Story of God Bible Commentary: Romans* (Grand Rapids: Zondervan, 2016), 3.
21. Moo, 73.
22. Pate, 46, 52.
23. Pate, 52-53.

24. Bird, 115.
25. Moo, 128.
26. Moo, 129.

Week 2: Good News About Hope

1. Bird, 145.
2. Strong's 3049, s.v. "logizomai," BibleStudyTools.com, https://www.biblestudytools .com/lexicons/greek/nas/logizomai.html.
3. Bird, 144.
4. Bird, 144.
5. Bird, 159.
6. Wiersbe, 53.
7. Wiersbe, 51.
8. Moo, 156.
9. Strong's 4102, s.v. "pistis," BibleStudyTools.com, https://www.biblestudytools.com /lexicons/greek/nas/pistis.html.
10. Strong's 1680, s.v. "elpis," BibleStudyTools.com, https://www.biblestudytools.com /lexicons/greek/nas/elpis.html.
11. Martin Luther, *Preface to the Letter of St. Paul to the Romans*, Christian Classics Ethereal Library, www.ccel.org/l/luther/romans/pref_romans.html.
12. Bird, quoting George Mueller, 154.
13. Bird, quoting Karl Barth in *Church Dogmatics*, II/1:460-461, 155.
14. Bird, 156.
15. Strong's 1515, s.v. "eirene," BibleStudyTools.com, https://www.biblestudytools.com /lexicons/greek/nas/eirene.html.
16. Wiersbe, 61.
17. Randy Alcorn, *Heaven* (Carol Stream, IL: Tyndale, 2004), 160.
18. Moo, 171.
19. Strong's 2644, s.v. "katallasso," BibleStudyTools.com, https://www.biblestudytools .com/lexicons/greek/nas/katallasso.html.
20. Major W. Ian Thomas, *The Saving Life of Christ* (Grand Rapids: Zondervan, 1961), 9.
21. Bird, 189. (Note: Some other sources attribute this quotation to Reinhold Niebuhr.)
22. Bird, 188.

Week 3: Good News About Daily Life

1. Moo, 200.
2. Pate, 148-149.
3. Wiersbe, 84.
4. "Hebrew Bible: Jewish Sacred Writings," Encyclopedia Britannica, https://www.britannica.com/topic/Hebrew-Bible.
5. Wiersbe, 86.
6. Moo, 241.
7. Moo, 237.
8. Francis Chan, *Forgotten God: Reversing Our Tragic Neglect of the Holy Spirit* (Colorado Springs: David C. Cook, 2009), 16.
9. Chan, 37.
10. Lisa Kepner, "Yates, Ira Griffith, Jr.," *Handbook of Texas Online*, Texas State Historical Association, https://tshaonline.org/handbook/online/articles/fyazp.

Week 4: Good News About God's Plan

1. Wiersbe, 112.
2. *The New Interpreter's Bible Commentary, Volume IX: Acts, Introduction to Epistolary Literature, Romans, 1 & 2 Corinthians, Galatians* (Nashville: Abingdon Press, 2015), 530.
3. Bird, 315.
4. Dennis Bratcher, ed., "The Five Articles of the Remonstrants (1610)," The Voice, CRI/Voice, Institute, http://www.crivoice.org/creedremonstrants.html.
5. Wiersbe, 119.
6. Strong's 3670, s.v. "homologeo," BibleStudyTools.com, https://www.biblestudytools.com/lexicons/greek/nas/homologeo.html.
7. Strong's 4100, s.v. "pisteuo," BibleStudyTools.com, https://www.biblestudytools.com/lexicons/greek/nas/pisteuo.html.
8. Moo, 302.
9. Strong's 1496, s.v. "egkentrizo," BibleStudyTools.com, https://www.biblestudytools.com/lexicons/greek/nas/egkentrizo.html.
10. Donald L. Wasson, "Pax Romana," Ancient History Encyclopedia, https://www.ancient.eu/Pax_Romana/.
11. Strong's 5485, s.v. "charis," BibleStudyTools.com, https://www.biblestudytools.com/lexicons/greek/kjv/charis.html.

12. Wiersbe, 140.

13. Wiersbe, 143.

Week 5: Good News About Relationships

1. Bird, 413.

2. Strong's 4964, s.v. "suschematizo," BibleStudyTools.com, https://www.biblestudytools .com/lexicons/greek/nas/suschematizo.html.

3. Strong's 3339, s.v. "metamorphoo," BibleStudyTools.com, https://www.biblestudytools .com/lexicons/greek/nas/metamorphoo.html.

4. Caroline Leaf, *Switch On Your Brain: The Key to Peak Happiness, Thinking, and Health* (Grand Rapids: Baker Books, 2013), 133–134.

5. Leaf, 19.

6. Moo, 404.

7. Moo, 414.

8. Moo, 409.

9. Bird, 444.

10. Bird, 442.

11. Bird, 449.

12. Bird, 448.

13. Bird, 458.

14. Philip Yancey, *What's So Amazing About Grace?* (Grand Rapids: Zondervan, 1997), 71.

15. "Dwight L. Moody, Quotes, Quotable Quote," Goodreads, https://www.goodreads .com/quotes/172011-out-of-100-men-one-will-read-the-bible-the.

16. Bird, 454.

17. Bird, 455.

18. "A Common Quotation from 'Augustine'?," posted by Steve Perisho, http://faculty .georgetown.edu/jod/augustine/quote.html.

Week 6: Good News About Eternity

1. See Pate, 291, and Gaebelein, 158.

2. See Wiersbe, 180.

3. NIBC, 655.

4. Moo, 504

Women's Bible Studies from
MELISSA SPOELSTRA

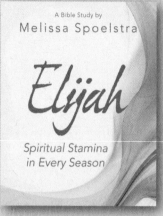

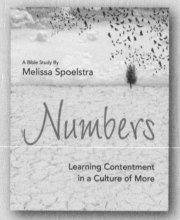

**Elijah: Spiritual Stamina
in Every Season**
Participant Workbook
9781501838910 | $16.99

**Numbers: Learning
Contentment in a Culture
of More**
Participant Workbook
9781501801747 | $16.99

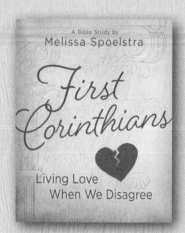

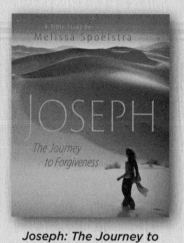

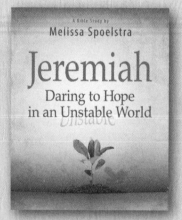

**First Corinthians: Living
Love When We Disagree**
Participant Workbook
9781501801686 | $15.99

**Joseph: The Journey to
Forgiveness**
Participant Workbook
9781426789106 | $15.99

**Jeremiah: Daring to Hope
in an Unstable World**
Participant Workbook
9781426788871 | $15.99

Leader guide, DVD, and Leader bundle
available for each Bible study.

Praise

"Melissa understands what it's like to be a woman who loves Jesus and still gets worn out from everyday life! She blew me away with her scriptural insight, creativity, and personal stories that deeply connect with my struggles. This study is a beautiful invitation for anyone who needs her tired, empty, or hurting soul to be filled and sustained by the limitless power of God."

—**Barb Roose,** author of *Winning the Worry Battle*
and the Bible study *Joshua: Winning the Worry Battle*

"Not only have I shared the stage with Melissa, but I also have had the privilege of sitting at her feet, so to speak, as she teaches the Word of God. It has been a blessing to see her passion ignite in us unity and a desire to love, serve, and study together. She is truly a powerhouse of the Holy Spirit!"

—**Mia Koehne**, Aspire Women's Events host, Worship Leader, Speaker, Singer Songwriter

Did you enjoy studying *Romans: Good News That Changes Everything*, or other studies by Melissa Spoelstra? Please share a review on your favorite online retailer site or social media platform.

Find samples and excerpts at AbingdonWomen.com.

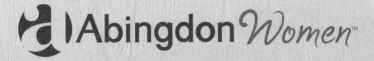

Books From
MELISSA SPOELSTRA

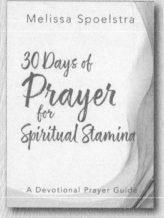

In *Dare to Hope*, Melissa Spoelstra draws upon her best-selling Bible study, *Jeremiah: Daring to Hope in an Unstable World,* to examine this hope-filled message, highlighting six guidelines for intentional living that enable us to overcome fear, worry, and doubt as we surrender to God and put our hope in Him alone.

Paperback | 9781501879654 | $16.99

Prayer is essential for developing spiritual stamina, and this prayer guide is intended to help you strengthen your prayer life and faith through a thirty-day prayer challenge. In it you will find prayer exercises offering instruction in a variety of prayer methods and approaches, including praying in silence, praying out loud, journaling your prayers, and drawing/coloring as you pray.

Paperback | 9781501874352 | $9.99

In *Total Family Makeover*, Melissa Spoelstra gives parents a way to build family discipleship. She focuses on eight key habits of growth—Spending Time in Prayer, Reading God's Word, Growing Through a Mentoring Relationship, Finding Community in the Church, Serving Others, Taking Time to Rest, Giving Back to God, and Sharing Your Faith—which offer a practical approach for your children to learn what it means to be a follower of Jesus.

Paperback | 9781501820656 | $16.99

In *Total Christmas Makeover* Melissa Spoelstra provides a practical approach for you and your family to turn your attention toward God's grace day by day as you prepare for Christmas. This 31-day devotional presents key scriptures, ideas to implement with each reading, and questions for reflection to guide you in rediscovering rituals, relationship, and rest—to connect you more deeply with Christ this holiday season.

Paperback | 9781501848704 | $16.99

If you enjoyed one of these books or a Bible study by Melissa Spoelstra, please share a review on your favorite online retailer site or social media platform.

AbingdonWomen.com